The Sun Never Sets

Bill Lane at the entrance of *Sunset* headquarters in 1989, upon his return from serving as U.S. ambassador to Australia.

The Sun Never Sets

Reflections on a Western Life

L. W. "Bill" Lane, Jr.

with Bertrand M. Patenaude,
and an Introduction by Kevin Starr

STANFORD GENERAL BOOKS
An Imprint of Stanford University Press
Stanford, California

Stanford University Press
Stanford, California

Library of Congress Cataloging-in-Publication Data

Lane, L. W., Jr. (Laurence William), 1919-2010, author.
   The sun never sets : reflections on a western life / L.W. "Bill" Lane, Jr. with Bertrand M. Patenaude ; and an Introduction by Kevin Starr.
       pages cm
   Includes index.
   ISBN 978-0-8047-8511-2 (cloth : alk. paper)
   1. Lane, L. W., Jr. (Laurence William), 1919-2010. 2. Publishers and publishing--California--Biography. 3. Ambassadors--United States--Biography. 4. *Sunset*--History.
I. Patenaude, Bertrand M., 1956- editor. II. Title.
   Z473.L284A3 2013
   070.5092--dc23
   [B]
                                        2012044740

ISBN 978-0-0847-8564-8 (electronic)

Designed by Bruce Lundquist
Typeset at Stanford University Press in 9/15 Stone Serif

Table of Contents

Introduction

Bill Lane's Reflections

by Kevin Starr

Autobiography is a literary form and a way of writing history. Like all literary forms, autobiography is selective. Even the most candid and comprehensive of autobiographies—for whatever reasons, including privacy and space available—must make choices regarding just exactly what should be told. In the case of *The Sun Never Sets: Reflections on a Western Life* by L. W. "Bill" Lane, Jr., autobiography and history converge. Bill Lane tells us his story of growing up in the Midwest, moving with his family to California, and becoming a citizen of the West, and also recounts, from the inside, the history of *Sunset* magazine, which under Lane family ownership became an enormously influential publication, and which made all of Bill's varied accomplishments possible, including this fascinating memoir.

Bill Lane's story began in Iowa and remained rooted in Midwestern values, but was transformed when his family relocated to California in 1928 after his father purchased *Sunset* magazine. That story then expanded into the Santa Clara Valley and the Yosemite Valley during Bill's teenage years and anchored itself in the travertine and russet-tiled cloisters of Stanford University, which for Bill Lane would always remain the emblem of his coming-of-age. Stanford also became an enduring symbol and catalyst for all that was best about the region he would uniquely make his own, especially once he took the helm of *Sunset* magazine.

That region extended from Iowa to the Bay Area to the Yosemite, to the Far West, and finally to the Asia/Pacific Basin, which Bill first encountered as a naval officer serving in the Second World War, and which he would later explore through travel and publication—indeed, helping to define the entire American relationship to this vast region. He capped this involvement by serving with great distinction as the U.S. ambassador to Australia in the 1980s, an episode he recounts in these pages.

The *Sunset* Saga

When Laurence W. Lane, Sr., stepped off the ferryboat at the foot of Market Street in mid-October 1928 after a long train ride from Iowa, a parade was in progress and the music of a great brass band filled the Ferry Terminal. All this was for Columbus Day, of course, but it might have been for Larry Lane as well, since a process was being set in motion—for the new publisher of *Sunset*, his wife, Ruth Bell Lane, and the two Lane sons, Laurence W. "Bill" Junior and Melvin Bell Lane—that would eventually present the Far West with its most successful magazine publisher and its most successful book publisher, from whom millions would learn how best to live in this still-new region.

Larry Lane had been advertising director of the Des Moines–based Meredith Publications, owner of the widely read *Better Homes and Gardens*, *Successful Farming*, and two other magazines. With the help of six other Des Moines investors, in September 1928 Lane purchased *Sunset*, which was struggling to survive, for $60,000.

The Southern Pacific Company had founded *Sunset* with the premier issue of May 1898, naming the magazine in honor of its crack overland Sunset Limited, which operated between New Orleans and Los Angeles. The Southern Pacific, in establishing *Sunset*, promoted travel and migration to the states it served. California provided a delightful destination for Easterners and Midwesterners eager to escape the wintry rigors of the East and Midwest via a luxurious transcontinental journey on the Sunset Limited to hotels on the shores of the Pacific.

Southern Pacific had sold the magazine in 1914 to a group of its editors, who refashioned it into a literary magazine, a kind of *Atlantic Monthly* of the West. In purchasing the magazine in 1928, Larry Lane had something quite different in mind. He formulated new editorial policies and recruited as senior editors two talented women from *Better Homes and Gardens* to help him implement those policies. *Sunset* had begun as a vehicle to promote the West as a place, for both settlement and travel. That orientation continued more vigorously than ever, but now it reflected Larry Lane's editorial credo that *Sunset* should be a practical, how-to-do-it magazine *for* the West, not simply *about* the West.

Like the *North American Review*, *Scribner's Monthly*, and the *New Yorker*, Lane's *Sunset* would help its readers define their intellectual preferences and tastes. Yet, also like the *Ladies' Home Journal*, the *Woman's Home Companion*, and *McCall's* magazine, *Sunset* would help them articulate and direct their emergent tastes, guiding them through a thousand domestic decisions.

Under Larry Lane, *Sunset* became a staff-written magazine with a tightly controlled editorial process. Regional coverage and editions played a key role in the new *Sunset*. As a magazine man from the Midwest, Larry Lane had become sensitive to just how important regional matters were to his readership—areas of gardening, home design, and home improvement were dependent on regional variation. Regional editions of the magazine, launched in 1932, helped *Sunset* weather the Great Depression, not only by opening the magazine to more focused articles but also by later bringing in local businesses as advertisers. In time, *Sunset* would carry more regional advertisements than any other magazine.

Larry Lane transformed *Sunset* into a family magazine by concentrating, always in a practical way, on four major editorial fields, which Bill Lane calls the "four wheels of the car": gardening, travel, home, and cooking. Like most other periodical publications in the 1930s, *Sunset* was struggling, but within the pages of the magazine there unfolded a panoramic pageant of gardening, architecture, regional cuisine, patio dining, golf, tennis, horseback riding, and other leisure pursuits, which represented, in its own way, a cunning strategy for economic success.

Bill's memoir makes plain that *Sunset* was a family-operated enterprise, with Dad at the helm and Mom advising throughout—especially, but not nearly exclusively, by testing recipes for publication in the magazine—and counseling the two female editors, who had been brought from Iowa and were part of the larger Lane family. Ruth Lane would step into the role of managing editor during and just after World War II. Young Bill and Mel, meanwhile, sold the magazine door-to-door, which marked the beginning of Bill's remarkable career as a salesman.

Returning from the service in 1946, the Lane brothers began an intense apprenticeship in every aspect of the publishing business. This was the moment when the magazine, like the West itself, was taking off. In the upcoming decades the Far West, California and Arizona especially, would add millions of new residents, brought there by a booming economy and the desire for a better life, one that was free of Eastern winters and offered new job opportunities.

Literally millions of new homes would be built; whole cities and suburbs would be created, almost overnight. Millions of Americans who were born and raised elsewhere would now be seeking to transform themselves into Far Westerners. What kinds of homes should they build? What foods should they prepare? What trees, shrubs, and flowers should they plant in their new environment? Where should they go on family vacations? *Sunset* began to answer these questions in its own way, and by 1947 circulation, which had remained in the 200,000s during the war, increased by 100,000, then reached 400,000 in 1948. For many years, the rate of *Sunset* circulation grew even faster than that of the population.

Sunset also began to publish books in a serious way. In 1946 its first large-format, hardcover book, *Western Ranch Houses*, appeared, written by *Sunset* editors with San Diego architect Cliff May and illustrated with May-designed houses. No single *Sunset* book before or since has had such a profound effect on the architectural environment of the Far West.

In 1951 Cliff May designed new headquarters for *Sunset* in Menlo Park, on the edge of San Francisquito Creek, and renowned landscape architect Thomas Church laid out the gardens. Church had invented the deck, first recognized in *Sunset* and perhaps the Far West's most notable contribution to domestic architecture after the Spanish-inspired patio.

In the flush and expectant years following the Second World War, *Sunset* had become more than a magazine. It had become a key prism through which the people of the Far West were glimpsing possibilities and futures for themselves and their region. For one thing, *Sunset* offered a continuous stream of practical solutions for home improvement and remodeling. The magazine's persistent preference was for homes that were simple and straightforward, devoid of historical fussiness, a style that can be generically described as California Ranch.

Ambience came from the emphasis on roofline, wall, mass, and volume in dialogue with, but not slavishly repeating, the best elements of the Southwestern and Southern Californian adobe. The concept of a home ranged across the entire space between property lines, encompassing both interior and exterior as a single living space. Here the garden became vitally important. As metaphor and ideal, the garden offered one of the most powerful images associated with the Far West in the nineteenth century. The search for the Garden of the West was central to the epic of Western settlement and migration.

In the treatment of food themes, both the magazine and the many cookbooks adhered to the usual philosophy of balance and practicality, the cycle of seasons, and family values promoted through cooking and eating together. *Sunset* editors emphasized the variety of fruits, vegetables, and dairy products in *Sunset* country. Certainly, *Sunset* played no small role in helping to revolutionize American cuisine—such a meat-and-potatoes affair in the nineteenth century—by featuring recipes starring garden vegetables and creatively fresh seasonings.

In each instance, in keeping with the *Sunset* editorial program, articles not only described the Far West but attracted readers to the region, as visitors or as settlers, in a most engaging and practical way. *Sunset* was interested in scenery for its own sake, true; but the magazine was also concerned with the human equation, in bringing scenery, flora, and fauna together with people in an atmosphere of respectful appreciation.

In its travel articles, *Sunset* consistently focused on nature and a family-oriented enjoyment of the outdoors—unlike typical travel guides, which would most likely emphasize archaeology or historical monuments. In the 1950s, in fact, accessible, family-friendly vacations became a popular topic of many travel articles published in *Sunset* magazine and books.

Sunset had entered the twentieth century primarily as a tourist magazine. *Sunset* in the second half of the twentieth century was a Far West institution, its Menlo Park headquarters a place of near-pilgrimage. Through *Sunset*, the Far West—now expanded to include the Mountain States, Hawaii, and Alaska—voiced its deepest hopes and dreams: its collective pursuit of happiness through an equally intense pursuit of the good life.

Bill Lane's memoir is especially insightful in its description of *Sunset*'s boom years after World War II, charting his own upward trajectory within the ranks of the magazine, as he becomes *Sunset*'s top advertising salesman, on the strength of a whirlwind eighteen months living and making business deals in midtown Manhattan. In 1959, while Larry Lane remained chairman of the board, Bill Lane became publisher of *Sunset* magazine, and Mel Lane assumed the direction of *Sunset* Books. It was a new and continuously expanding era. In 1967 alone *Sunset* Books sold an astonishing 1.5 million copies.

Sunset was concerned with proper stewardship, use, and enjoyment of the environment: a direct continuity of its Progressive heritage. Hence, *Sunset*'s continuing interest in national parks, places of natural beauty set aside specifically for human enjoyment. After Bill and Mel Lane took over for their father, *Sunset* had even more of an influence on shaping the way people lived in the Far West and exercised their stewardship of the environment. *Sunset* readers were encouraged to learn to live with nature, side by side, and to partake of nature's gifts in a respectful, caring manner.

With the enthusiastic support of Bill and Mel Lane and their editors, *Sunset* magazine, books, and films advanced a steady, if occasionally subtle, program of conservation advocacy. In the February 1979 issue celebrating fifty years of Lane ownership, *Sunset* took pride in its role in advocating environmental living, leading-edge technology, the new agriculture and aquaculture, good nutrition, preservationism, and public parks. These concerns were then reflected in articles on traffic, open space, waste management, urban design, water conservation, and other social and environmental matters.

By 1990, when Bill and Mel sold *Sunset* to Time Warner, the magazine's values and interests had become ingrained in the mentality of its sizable and influential readership, and in the wider culture.

The Lane Family

While *The Sun Never Sets* is not an overly personal or even psychological narrative, it is obvious throughout this memoir just how much Bill Lane loved his family, respected and befriended his colleagues, and worked alongside high-ranking officials of every sort in a spirit of non-partisanship. In this regard Bill's brother, Mel, younger by two years, holds special status. A reader of this narrative loses count of the times that Bill Lane acknowledges his creative and vibrant partnership with his brother. Were ever two brothers so successfully joined throughout a lifetime in such a trailblazing enterprise as *Sunset* became?

Likewise, this memoir is a tribute of a son to parents who raised their sons according to what we like to think of as traditional American values and, when the time came, turned over to them the enterprise that had been the all-consuming work of their own lives. The vignettes of family life that Bill Lane recounts here are classic American scenes, right out of a novel by Booth Tarkington, and so are his memories of hard work demanded and challenges met. Larry and Ruth Lane cherished their boys and gave them an abundance of love and support but refused to coddle them in any manner whatsoever. From the beginning, the boys worked, and worked hard, learning life and the magazine business from the ground up. Can there be any more dramatic example of starting at the bottom of a business—literally from the ground floor—than Bill Lane's account of taking off his naval officer's uniform at the end of the war and assuming command of the elevator at the *Sunset* headquarters in downtown San Francisco? Far from being bitter over the homecoming assignment, Bill Lane—who had recently served on an admiral's staff as a full lieutenant after sea service in the Pacific—seemed rather proud of this brief but symbolic postwar apprenticeship.

Equally charming is his account of his courtship of Donna Jean Gimbel, a graduate of Northwestern University, whom he briefly dated in Chicago before her move to California, where they resumed their friendship, which developed into much more: marriage and family in the 1950s, a time when young Americans in droves were moving west, and marrying, and starting families, and building or buying homes, and providing *Sunset* with a rapidly expanding readership as they explored for themselves the promise of Western Living. As in the case of his parents and his brother, Bill Lane brings his wife and children into this narrative—not at great length, certainly, but in vignettes, snapshots even, that show them pursuing and enjoying the good life at the high tide of the American Century.

The *Sunset* Family

Like his father and brother, Bill Lane was a businessman, and a very good one at that. He could be demanding, and he knew how to say no, especially when it came to what kind of advertising *Sunset* would carry or what kind of stories it would run. Yet fifty to sixty years after the postwar *Sunset* culture was fully established by the Lane brothers, we can admire the family nature of the business, so vividly described by Bill in his memoir. Here was a time in the American economy when those who owned companies not only invested in them, or bought and sold them, but ran them personally and created among their employees a cooperative spirit, a sense of solidarity and belonging akin to family. Here, too, *Sunset* was on the cutting edge.

To work at *Sunset* during these years was to enjoy a career connected to a meaningful enterprise as well as to earn a livelihood. With few exceptions, employees remained on the job for twenty, thirty, or even more years. Innumerable times in this narrative, Bill Lane recognizes and praises editors and staffers—even one very talented, albeit contrarian, editor who did not fit into the *Sunset* ethos and was asked to retire. There was no such thing as layoffs, for the Lane brothers kept income and expenses in tight alignment. They took from the enterprise a good living but felt no need to squeeze it dry. *Sunset* was, after all, a family company. If an employee was facing a financial difficulty, the Lanes discreetly helped out. The very headquarters that Cliff May designed for *Sunset* recapitulated the design and feel of a family home in the Spanish colonial style, California Ranch, a national favorite by the 1960s. At Christmastime, Bill Lane—who prided himself on his abilities as an actor and speaker—played Santa Claus for employees' children, arriving by fire truck or, on one occasion, by helicopter.

Midwestern Origins and Influences

The entire Lane saga, as Bill Lane tells it, is permeated by Midwestern people, places, and values. Larry Lane was born in Kansas. Bill Lane's beloved grandmother, in Illinois. His mother was born in Iowa; his wife, Illinois. Ruth Bell Lane's father served as president of Drake University, where Ruth and Larry met and married following graduation. Larry Lane's career was shaped and facilitated by Iowa-based magazines such as *Successful Farming* and *Better Homes and Gardens*. Bill and Mel Lane were raised on a small farm outside Des Moines, where they were responsible for routine farm chores, including milking the family cow, a skill in which Bill Lane took pride for a lifetime. On the farm there was a pony and a German shepherd named Cleta, who moved to California along with the Lane family. Bill Lane's recollections of growing up in such an environment are reminiscent of Tom Sawyer: the farm and its animals, walking to school along a train track, his mother's pride in her garden, Larry Lane away on sales trips, then returning to the family with supplies of such surprising new foods as avocados, oranges, and brussels sprouts, which his mother learned to prepare for the family table.

Within the framework of autobiography, Bill Lane is remembering these things and telling us about them because he is also defining for himself and for us the origins of the *Sunset* mystique: its focus on home life, on work around the home and garden, and, underlying all of this, the promise of American life as expressed in places such as Iowa, where the Lane family lived, or Minnesota, where the Lanes vacationed, or Kansas and Illinois, where the Lane parents had been born and come of age.

To be happy at home, Dr. Samuel Johnson once remarked, can be considered the end of all human endeavor. Bill Lane wants us—and himself—to realize that he understood this point of view from personal experience, and it animated such magazines as *Better Homes and Gardens*, for which his father then worked, and *Sunset*, which he would soon acquire and revitalize.

As a family, the Lanes were not exempt from struggle and disappointment, of course, but that is not what Bill Lane wants to talk about. Rather, he wants to relate the story of what the family enjoyed, the values and pursuits that held it together, and the way that those values and pursuits, centered on the home and on family, radiated outward into a larger message, which formed the basis for an impressively successful magazine.

California Dreams

In the late nineteenth and early twentieth centuries, this Midwestern point of view was translated wholesale to California, especially Southern California, as a generation of Midwesterners migrated west, among them Bill Lane's maternal grandparents and his mother's four brothers, all of whom moved to Los Angeles in 1919 as an advance guard for subsequent Lane migration. This influx of Midwesterners into Southern California constituted the determining social dynamic of the first three decades of the twentieth century. It began in the 1880s with affluent Midwesterners who were attracted to Southern California for the climate. Initially, they came on a seasonal basis to escape the brutal winters of the Midwest. Then many of them decided to stay, and by the early 1900s they had upgraded Southern California with the establishment of colleges—Pomona, for example, where Bill Lane spent his freshman and sophomore years before transferring to Stanford, as well as USC, Whittier, and Occidental—along with multiple churches, choral groups, and the beginnings of the Hollywood Bowl.

Midwesterners came to Northern California as well, albeit in smaller numbers. More than half the population of the state at this time lived in the San Francisco Bay Area, and San Francisco itself, an international city since the Gold Rush, had one of the highest ratios of foreign to native-born residents. Still, even Northern California, the Bay Area especially, experienced certain changes and developments as a result of this in-migration from the heartland. The newly founded Stanford University, for example, recruited its first president, David Starr Jordan, from Indiana, as well as a number of its founding faculty from the Midwest, and the first student to present himself for registration was a young Iowan by the name of Herbert Hoover.

By the time the Lanes arrived in San Francisco in 1928—Larry Lane in October via railroad, Ruth and their sons in December, chauffeured there from Iowa in the family Packard, its sideboards stacked with luggage—Midwesterners and Midwestern values had taken strong hold in the Golden State. Long Beach, for example, was known as Iowa by the Sea, and Los Angeles County had so many resettled Iowans living there that each year they gathered in Long Beach on a county-by-county basis, some 25,000 strong, for wholesale picnicking and attendant festivities.

Midwesterners and Midwestern values helped bring the Progressive movement to California, indeed, transformed California into one of the most Progressive states of the nation along with Illinois and New York. In 1907 California Progressives organized the Lincoln Roosevelt League, with the express intention of reforming the state. By the legislative session of 1911, Progressives were in control of the governorship and the legislature, and under the direction of Governor Hiram Johnson, they recast state government for the next hundred years.

Bill Lane was suspicious of labels. He was even more suspicious of ideologies, as opposed to bedrock beliefs and values. Hence in later years he resisted—if ever so subtly—an identification of *Sunset*, even the pre-Lane *Sunset*, with "Progressivism" spelled with a capital *P*. This designation, in Bill's opinion, could too easily be confused with "progressivism" with a small *p*, as in current usage, suggesting a left-liberal orientation. Still, whatever Bill Lane's difficulties with the term, the *Sunset* venture, once the Southern Pacific detached itself from ownership, embodied early twentieth-century Progressive values anchored in and intensified by a Midwestern preference for good government, environmentalism, and a general sense of stewardship that promoted the good life for the greatest number of citizens possible. Although Larry Lane steered *Sunset* away from politics and Bill and Mel Lane continued that tradition, a bipartisan Progressive message, suffused with Midwestern values, animated the *Sunset* point of view. Life, land, home, and garden should be appreciated, celebrated, and nurtured. The ability to do this implied that synthesis of private and public value so evident in Bill Lane's later years as he assumed appointive responsibilities on the state, national, and international levels.

The post–Southern Pacific *Sunset* reflected Progressive values linked to responsible and aesthetic living in a regional context, which was one of the reasons it so attracted Larry Lane. He intensified this dimension of the magazine even as he pruned back other kinds of coverage, refashioning *Sunset* into a lifestyle magazine openly concerned with the aesthetic, an orientation even further developed by Bill and Mel Lane and the talented staff that they assembled in the postwar era. Notice how frequently Bill Lane refers to aesthetic value in this memoir. For the settings of life—home, garden, hearth, and kitchen—to flourish, moreover, there had to be a proper and efficiently functioning society that would serve as a sustaining context. The more *Sunset* focused on domestic living, the more important this larger context became, and over time this orientation led Bill Lane further into public service. No home, no garden exists in isolation.

The very advertising carried by *Sunset* served the flourishing economy that was also necessary alongside a rightly ordered public sector. Local, state, national, and international well-being was implied as *Sunset* expanded its concept of Western living to include the Northwest, the Southwest, the Mountain States, Alaska, Hawaii, and the Asia/Pacific Basin. Spiraling upward with *Sunset*, Bill Lane was approached for cabinet office, which he declined, held the rank of ambassador as well as other important federal and state appointments, but also served as the first mayor of his hometown, Portola Valley, a community near Stanford that he helped bring into being and design as a civic entity.

Yosemite, Stanford, and the West

This memoir opens and closes with recollections of the first visit of the Lane family to Yosemite, in the summer of 1929. Throughout his life, Bill Lane was sustained by the memory of that boyhood experience.

In the early 1860s, the Unitarian minister Thomas Starr King of San Francisco urged Californians to build within themselves "Yosemites of the soul," which is to say, to take Yosemite as the reality and symbol of all that California—as place, people, and society—promised in the way of social and spiritual development. Bill Lane would never have expressed himself in such grandiloquent terms, but he does describe for us on a number of occasions the thrill of a boy from the flatlands of Iowa at first beholding the soaring granite walls of the Yosemite Valley. He also relates in some detail his early employment in the valley and beyond as a packer of horses and mules for trips into the high country, as well as, later, the member of the Camp Curry staff responsible for calling out, "Let the fire fall!" signaling the descent of a cascade of gleaming coals from Glacier Point while a female vocalist sang Rudolf Friml's "Indian Love Call." Indeed, well into his eighth decade Bill Lane, upon request and in the proper circumstances, would repeat this stentorian call in honor of a firefall that was now impossible because of the environmental movement in which he had played such a prominent part.

So, too, did Stanford University, along with Yosemite, embody for Bill Lane not only the memory and promise of his college days as a fraternity man, aspiring actor, student publications manager, and all-round Stanford man in corduroy pants, V-neck sweater, and saddle shoes, but also the promise of California and the West, as well as the stewardship that these regions deserved and received from Stanford and Stanford alumni. A product of the Palo Alto public schools in their golden age, including the legendary Palo Alto High School of the prewar era, Bill Lane matured intellectually and imaginatively in the shadow of Stanford and all that Stanford represented, and in later years, in symbiosis with *Sunset*, Stanford for him was linked in memory and service with the best possibilities of the West. Over the years, Bill and Jean Lane contributed generously to Stanford—in the restoration of the original Quadrangle, for example—and the most notable of their gifts to Stanford established an institute devoted to the study and advocacy of the very same West that had not only produced Stanford but also accounted for the success of *Sunset* itself.

Asia/Pacific Basin

The *Sunset* acquired by Larry Lane in 1928 was California-oriented, and the writers and artists of the magazine through the 1930s, as well as their editorial preoccupations, were California-oriented as well. In the immediate postwar era, California received the bulk of the American population heading west, but rather soon this westward tilt also began to populate the Southwest, the Northwest, and the Mountain States, all of which became zoned territory for *Sunset* coverage. Likewise, the territories of Alaska and Hawaii were appropriated as *Sunset* country. Even before World War II, however, *Sunset* was adding to its repertoire—at least through advertising, and through some coverage as well—the Far East, especially Japan. Just as *Sunset*, both the magazine and the books, helped to define Southern California—followed by comparable definitions of other Western regions—the expansion of coverage by the publications to include the Asia/Pacific Basin, gathering momentum from the 1960s onward, documented and fostered a growing awareness of that area as the Mediterranean of the twenty-first century.

Bill Lane was instrumental in helping to generate this wave—and he rode it to personal success and recognition. Among his many accomplishments, he played a major role in founding the Pacific Area Travel Association. In 1975 he served as high commissioner with the rank of ambassador to the International Exposition on Okinawa, where the Lanes spent an entire year, an experience that he recalls fondly in these pages. Bill Lane's nomination by President Ronald Reagan in 1985 to serve as ambassador to Australia and the Republic of Nauru brought to Canberra an experienced public servant who had a long association with the region. After all, in 1978 and 1980 *Sunset* Books had published widely popular travel guides to Australia and New Zealand, annexing them across the Pacific as *Sunset* country. As ambassador, Bill Lane served during the final years of the Cold War, when the United States Navy stood in danger of losing its ability to operate its nuclear-powered ships freely in the South Pacific.

Working on behalf of American interests in the area, Lane showed a bulldog tenacity and a steely resolve that was one part of his nature, albeit frequently masked by his sunny disposition. At the same time, he communicated to Australians his love for their island continent and his recognition of the debt that California owed Australia in matters as diverse as eucalyptus trees and irrigation engineering, as well as the similarities and convergences of the Australian and Western American lifestyles. When Ambassador Lane, in full Western gear, including a ten-gallon hat, rode in an Australian parade, Australians readily understood that the ambassador was alluding to two comparable frontiers on two sides of the Pacific and recalling the horsemen who had driven cattle across comparable plains.

Salesman . . . and Horseman

The realistic, hard-nosed side to Bill Lane that made him such an effective Cold War ambassador was rarely evident, as by and large he maintained a pervasively genial demeanor. Bill was the kind of man who could openly speak of his love of home, family, and country. He was regularly courteous and caring—and smiling. But he was also a shrewd and effective businessman.

Bill Lane was proud to call himself a salesman: someone who had something good to sell—a way of life and travel, a way of conservation and stewardship—and he was proud to sell it. As a salesman, he spoke effectively. But like any good salesman, he also knew how to listen. Listening closely and persistently, he and his brother, Mel, like their parents before them, came to understand certain dreams connected to the American West: dreams of a better life, enhanced by efficiency and beauty, attuned to private, public, and institutional values. This memoir suggests the range and depth of Bill Lane's involvement in the people, places, and causes he loved and worked on behalf of throughout a long and productive life, well spent in the cause of Western living.

For Bill, the most powerful symbol of it all—of his move from the Midwest, his new circumstances in the West, the possibilities that lay before him—was the figure of the horse (as it was for the young protagonist of John Steinbeck's *The Red Pony*). Bill was even more passionate about horses than about salesmanship. He would love and cherish and ride horses, with great skill, across a lifetime. As varied and successful as this man's life became, as filled with achievements and affiliations as it was, Bill Lane always loved riding and continued to list it, along with hiking, as his lifetime hobbies. Perhaps the most iconic image this memoir suggests is that of Bill on horseback, reveling in the interactivity of man and horse, landscape and sky, the promise and magic of a life lived to the fullest in the American West.

Editor's Note

Bill Lane decided to begin writing his memoirs in the autumn of 2008, shortly after his eighty-ninth birthday. On the strength of our mutual Stanford associations, Bill asked me to help him with the task. The process began with a series of audiotaped interviews conducted at his home in Portola Valley and, on one occasion, at his summer home at Lake Tahoe. These interviews were supplemented, and greatly facilitated, by frequent consultation of a printed copy of an extensive oral history that Bill had given to Bancroft Library's Regional Oral History Office (ROHO) in 1993 and 1994. Those interviews, expertly conducted by Suzanne Riess, proved to be an invaluable resource for refreshing Bill's memory and were an essential foundation for the writing of this memoir (ROHO interviews with Proctor Mellquist and Walter Doty, as part of the Thomas Church oral history project, were also helpful). Other essential building blocks were Bill's extensive private archive of speeches, photographs, and memorabilia, as well as *Sunset*-related correspondence written by Bill and by his father, Laurence William Lane, Sr.

Bill Lane was keen to have his memoir elucidate his life beyond *Sunset*—his service as a naval officer during the Second World War, his committee work in Washington, D.C., in the 1970s, his diplomacy as ambassador-at-large to Japan in 1975–76 and U.S. ambassador to Australia from 1985 to 1989, his environmentalism, his love of horses. Always, though, the memoir, like the man, remained tethered to *Sunset*, which, along with (indeed often inseparable from) his family, was the center of his life.

Bill made it clear from the outset that he did not want his memoir to bore people with personal family details. The one family member whom he was concerned to discuss fully and fairly was his younger brother, business partner, and fellow environmentalist, Mel. Mel Lane complemented Bill at *Sunset* with his formidable creative and management skills, which were responsible for making *Sunset* Books such a huge success. Whereas Bill welcomed the limelight, Mel preferred to remain in the background.

As a result, Bill, with his larger-than-life personality and booming baritone voice to match, became the face of *Sunset*. As he composed this memoir, Bill kept checking with his editor to make sure that he was giving brother Mel his due.

Throughout Bill's time at *Sunset*, from his postwar apprenticeship through his years as publisher of the magazine, he was used to playing multiple roles on both the editorial and the business sides. These included the role of editor, an avocation he continued to practice as a memoirist. He was constantly revising the wording of his text and, like many writers, found it difficult to decide that a chapter was finished and to part with it. He was editing the final draft of the manuscript almost to the end, which came on July 31, 2010—Bill Lane's last "closing date."

Bill's widow, Jean, and the Lane children—Sharon, Bob, and Brenda—in keeping with Bill's wishes, have enthusiastically supported the publication of this memoir. The project was also aided by the contributions of Joan Lane, Donald C. Meyer, Jack Morton, Charles Palm, Bill Marken, Floyd Shaw, René Klein, Lauren Dunbar, Spencer Toy, Barb Newton, Donald Lamm, and especially by the efforts of Bill's secretary of nearly thirty years, Karen Hamilton.

Bertrand M. Patenaude
Stanford University

The Sun Never Sets

Bill Lane in 1921, when he was eighteen months old.

Chapter 1

Columbus Day

The Heartland of the Midwest

Some of my earliest memories of growing up in Iowa have to do with the cold. Apart from snowstorms and sledding, I remember ice cream bars, and plenty of them. During that period, my father worked at Meredith Publishing Company, in Des Moines, publisher of *Successful Farming* and *Better Homes and Gardens*. In the early 1920s Dad was personnel manager, and he had the company cafeteria as part of his bailiwick.

One day a man came in with a proposition about an ice cream bar. Dad thought maybe he had a good idea, and he talked to my mother about it. She developed a dark chocolate sauce that would freeze, and they cut up frozen ice cream, dipped it into the sauce, and put a stick in it. Then they put a wrapper on it. My father organized a little investment group and got this fellow to agree to syndicate what they named the Eskimo Pie. You would sell the wrappers, and of course the franchisee would have to adhere to the recipe and the promotions and advertising and so forth. They never got any legal documents to obligate this entrepreneur who came up with the original concept, but it was my dad's marketing idea to franchise these wrappers as a way of controlling the distribution and getting a royalty, because you sold the wrappers.

The dark chocolate was the key food ingredient, and as I say, my mother came up with the recipe for it. She did the testing in our kitchen where we lived, in our house in Des Moines. I remember the testing that went on when I was a very small kid, with this group of grown-ups sitting around the table tasting these ice cream bars. I've always been interested in ice cream bars. I became one of the biggest Häagen-Dazs ice cream bar fans around. And it all started, at least in part, because of that Eskimo Pie.

This episode, which I now can only hazily recall, exemplifies the kind of collaboration between Mom and Dad that would become a hallmark of the Lane family.

My father, Laurence Lane, was born in Horton, Kansas, in 1890. His father, William Earl Lane, died when my dad was two. My father's mother, Estella Louise Lane, was from a farming family background in Geneseo and Moline, Illinois. After his father's death, my father went back with his mother to live with relatives in northern Illinois.

He and his mother struggled to get by. She had a boardinghouse that I remember going to as a child in the early 1920s, before we moved to California in 1928. Dad had to work for everything, and when he was sixteen

Laurence and Ruth Lane in Palm Springs in 1937.

he dropped out of high school in order to take a job. For a time he worked as a hardware salesman, jogging around Minnesota in a horse and buggy selling Keen Kutter knives. He later went back to school and completed his remaining two years of high school in a single year, in 1913, when he turned twenty-three. He then moved to Iowa with his mother and enrolled at Drake University.

While at Drake, Larry Lane went to work part-time and summers for the Meredith Publishing Company. It was the beginning of a publishing career that would last well beyond a half century. At Drake, his normal bent for knowledge was somewhat distracted by a first-class extracurricular interest: the daughter of the university president, Dr. Hill McClelland Bell, who served as Drake's president from 1903 to 1918.

Mom's background was radically different from Dad's. Born in Lincoln, Nebraska, she grew up in an academician's home. Dad was a good student, but Mom was the more natural student. She was a home economics major and Phi Beta Kappa. Years later, Mom served on Drake's board of trustees. Their romance and graduation were enhanced during senior year by Mom being elected "Queen of the May" by the graduating men students, while Dad was elected "Cardinal" by the Women's League for the annual May Festival.

Ruth Bell and Larry Lane were married right after graduation, which happened to be just at the time that the United States entered the First World War, in the spring of 1917. Dad joined the army, commissioned as a first lieutenant. Mom accompanied him to Fort Oglethorpe, in Georgia, where he did psychiatric screening for draftees to determine whether they were capable or qualified for war duty.

After the war, Dad returned to Meredith, where he served as personnel manager for *Successful Farming*, a practically oriented, how-to magazine, aimed equally at the Midwestern farming husband and wife. *Successful Farming* was a regional magazine. It catered to what back then was called "The Heartland of the Midwest," covering about ten Midwestern states.

Moving up the ladder, Dad then became assistant advertising manager for *Better Homes and Gardens*, established by Meredith in 1922 as *Fruit, Garden & Home* and renamed two years later. Before long, he became advertising director for all the Meredith publications. The flagship was the very successful *Better Homes and Gardens*. I have no doubt that my mother's inspiration and her interests—her love of gardening and food—influenced my father a great deal, and had a lot to do with his interest in *Better Homes and Gardens* and the direction it took in the 1920s. The new magazine was aimed at the home and gardening family, and every article provided an affirmative answer to the question "Is it possible to do something as a result

3

of reading this article?" This was a test that Larry Lane was later to apply to the articles published in his own magazine.

I was born in an apartment down in the city of Des Moines, but very shortly after that my parents built the home on Hickman Road, a dirt and gravel road outside Des Moines. It was a very small, unpretentious house, way out in the country back then, and by now long gone. My brother, Mel, was born two and a half years later. I associate that house with some Airedales we had when I was a small boy. I remember throwing a little Airedale puppy off the sofa and my brother catching it. At least one of those Airedales grew up in our family, because I can recall a big Airedale in the backseat of our car, and my dad instructing me to hang on to it. Of course I did, and when the dog jumped out of the car, it took me along with it.

We had a small farm, with a cow, a pig, and some chickens. I had early exposure to farm life, and in fact one of my earliest memories is of milking a cow. Mom had a very extensive vegetable garden. And we had a pony, a little black pinto named Betty, and a wonderful dog called Cleta, a German shepherd that lived to be very old.

I remember going to school, walking along the streetcar tracks leading out of Des Moines. I went up through the sixth or seventh grade in the suburb. Memories grow fuzzy, but landmark events help make them vivid. I can't think of the name of my early grammar school now, but I remember the day of Charles Lindbergh's historic landing of the *Spirit of St. Louis* in

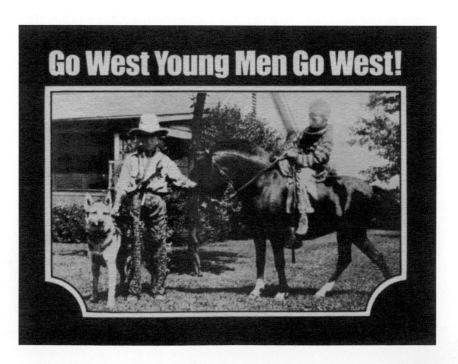

Go West Young Men Go West!

Bill (standing) and Mel Lane, with pony Betty and dog Cleta, at their home in Iowa.

Paris. It was May 21, 1927, a Saturday. Mel and I sat in the driveway listening to telegraph reports sent from Paris by Atlantic cable on earphones on a little squawk box, a forerunner of early radio called a "crystal set."

Lindbergh's flight was a benchmark in my interest in aviation, which began very early at a wonderful Iowa State Fair that Mom and Dad took us to, an annual event with lots of exhibits, mostly agriculture, of course. I remember a big room that was definitely refrigerated because it had life-size sculptures of a cow, a farmer, and his wife, all sculpted in solid butter. One of the major attractions that particular year was a Ford Trimotor plane that did a loop. That certainly made a big impression on me.

Given my father's work, I was heavily exposed to magazines, especially those put out by Meredith, a company run like a family by its founder and president, Edwin Meredith. From everything I can recall and from what I later learned from listening to my father, it was a wonderful place to work. I went with my parents to Christmas parties down at Meredith where the company gave away five-pound boxes of candy—five pounds!—to all employees. I remember holding this big, thick box of candy. The family atmosphere at Meredith had a strong influence on Dad, and through him on me and my younger brother, Mel. It would help shape the kind of company he would soon establish, a company that he, and then Mel and I as his successors, would manage in the coming decades.

Our family did a lot of vacation camping up in Minnesota, once near Lake Minnetonka, so we had a great deal of experience being outdoors and enjoying each other's company in natural surroundings. We never traveled as a family to New England, to the South, or to Europe. But through Meredith, and through some family connections, we had a steady exposure to life in the American West.

In the growth years of the Roaring Twenties, Dad traveled around the country setting up sales offices and fulfilling special assignments for Mr. Meredith on *Better Homes and Gardens* and *Successful Farming*. These assignments often took him west, especially to California, Oregon, and Washington, to drum up advertising. He called on the Raisin Advisory Board, Del Monte, and the Washington Apple Advisory Board, among other food entities. Down in Los Angeles there were several advertising accounts, including Southern California tourism organizations that wanted to promote tourism from the Midwest.

Dad soon learned from his travels and from talking with readers and analyzing reader letters that the greatest difference in living, and in attitudes towards living, were evident when he crossed the Mississippi and traveled over the Western states to the Pacific Ocean. The opportunities, as well as the problems, of building, caring for, and enjoying a home and garden were very different in the Western communities of Salt Lake City, Pasadena, Palo Alto, and Tacoma from what they were along the Des Moines River.

Dad also observed another major difference between Eastern and Western America. In the days of train travel, the itinerant businessman usually saw a big spread of countryside between destinations in the West. Trips were longer and many a weekend was spent sightseeing far from home—particularly in the Far West, where there was such a variety of things to see. The availability of year-round travel and outdoor recreation, fast accelerating with the increasing ownership of automobiles, became very apparent to Larry Lane, Corn Belt salesman, as he rode over virtually every mile of rail line west of the Rockies.

After a business trip, he'd bring home supplies of avocados, oranges, and brussels sprouts to his curious family in Des Moines. These wonders had a magical effect on young boys growing up in Iowa. I was very conscious of our limited supply of fresh vegetables in winter. Mom had a root cellar in the basement. I would go down into that cold basement when it was freezing outside, and here were turnips, carrots, potatoes, and other root plants you could store in a basement. The possibilities were limited, of course, so my dad's return from California with, say, a supply of fresh brussels sprouts, was a cause for wonder.

I remember Dad once coming back with a crate of artichokes. We used to meet his train at the station in Moline, because the train didn't go through Des Moines. He walked up with this crate of something very exotic-looking. At that time, Mom had never seen an artichoke—or if she had, she certainly had never cooked one. What on earth do you do with an artichoke? Such ingredients were not available in Iowa, so there was no way to write about them in *Better Homes and Gardens*, even though the magazine had a national audience. Still, Mom became intrigued with the possibilities of Western cooking.

Anyway, Dad had plenty of opportunity to witness the striking contrasts between the Midwest and the West, and not only in winter. Of the thousands of miles of track that he covered, perhaps none was more significant than a seventy-one-mile excursion on the Yosemite Valley Railroad. The year was 1922. Mr. Meredith invited him along on a ride through the San Joaquin Valley as the guest of the president of the Southern Pacific Railroad, who provided his private car. Dad loved to recall this trip, and it has become legendary in our family.

Mr. Meredith had served as secretary of agriculture under President Woodrow Wilson, and the traveling group included experts on the agricultural economy of the great San Joaquin Valley. As a sidelight, they switched off the main line and rattled up the spectacular valley of the Merced River to the El Portal Terminal, in the Sierra Nevada foothills and the mountains, where they transferred to a motorized open bus for the drive into Yosemite Valley. The dramatic transition from seacoast to broad valley to high mountains in only a few hours' travel made a lasting impression on Dad and convinced him that travel and recreation would, in the advancing age of the automobile, play an increasingly significant role in the lives of Western families.

Westward Ho!

It wasn't long before Mom, Mel, and I got to see the magical West for ourselves, as our family branched out to the coast. My mother's father had gotten diabetes and retired as president of Drake University in 1918, and he and Grandma Bell and Mom's four brothers moved to Southern California, to Los Angeles, and a house off Wilshire Boulevard in 1919, the year I was born.

This move west was hardly an unusual phenomenon. Midwesterners migrated to Southern California in large numbers in the early years of the twentieth century. Land was subdivided and was sold very cheap to get the population to move out to the West in order to develop a consumer base for agriculture and for other business. Iowans certainly did their part. For a time, Long Beach was informally known as "Little Iowa" and "Iowa-by-the-Sea."

The cover of the inaugural issue of *Sunset* magazine, May 1898.

The Southern Pacific Railroad had a tremendous vested interest in this. Synonymous with the West in 1898, the S.P. was then the major transportation system, landholder, Washington lobbyist, and, by all odds, the West's greatest booster for agricultural, industrial, and tourism development. For over three decades, the "Big Four" of Huntington, Stanford, Hopkins, and Crocker pyramided an empire that had no peer west of the Great Divide and few in the entire country. Desiring a publication to serve as the voice of that empire, the Southern Pacific created *Sunset* magazine in honor of its crack overland train, operating between New Orleans and Los Angeles, the *Sunset Limited*. It still operates today.

Founded in 1898, *Sunset* had an explicit creed: "Its aims are the presentation, in a

VOL. I. MAY, 1898. NO. 1.

YOSEMITE AND THE HIGH SIERRA IN THIS NUMBER.

convenient form, of information concerning the great states of California, Oregon, Nevada, Texas, Louisiana, and the territories of Arizona and New Mexico—a rich and inexhaustible field over which the dawn of future commercial and industrial importance is just breaking." The Southern Pacific used the pages of *Sunset* to lure people, especially those east of the Mississippi, to come west and buy land. *Sunset* was in part a society magazine, featuring articles about natural wonders like Yosemite but also chatty stories from places like Los Angeles, Santa Cruz, and Paso Robles. The magazine offered news about mining and farming, as well as poetry and jokes, always in the spirit of the *Sunset* motto: "Publicity for the attractions and advantages of the Western Empire."

Sunset was based in San Francisco, and published articles about the city's April 1906 earthquake and the rapid recovery in the years afterward. No natural disaster could dampen the enthusiasm for the migration to the West. The *Sunset* issues of these years, printed on the Southern Pacific's own presses, were filled with advertisements for nearly every Western county and irrigation district, wooing settlers to a land where everyone could strike it rich and have an orange tree and a palm tree in the front yard as well. In the April 1910 issue, land in the Fresno area—"California's Valley of the Nile"—was advertised at $40 to $125 an acre, with a small cash payment and the balance to be paid over four years.

These were the years when the Western states, and particularly California, experienced some of the largest percentage gains in population ever recorded. Many of the new Westerners were enticed here by the seductive pages of *Sunset*. Most of the newcomers crossed the plains and mountains by train. Many arrived by ship, and the S.P. had some of that action, too, as it controlled a major steamship line with connections with Eastern and world ports, including Hawaii.

In 1912 *Sunset* acquired *Pacific Monthly*, a magazine also founded in 1898, in Portland, Oregon. Largely supported by railroad interests to promote the Pacific Northwest, its format was similar to *Sunset*'s, its mission in life was identical, and, combined, the two magazines blanketed the Far West. For many years after the merger, although *Sunset* used numerous subtitles, the "Pacific Monthly" subtitle was legally protected, and during the decades the magazine was under Lane ownership you would find it on the contents page of every issue.

It was no more than a decade later, in the early 1920s, that our family began visiting my mom's family in Southern California and got to see for ourselves the territory that my dad had begun to imagine as his own. We came out from Iowa in the summers, and sometimes over Christmas. Virtually every year we rode the Rio Grande Railroad out to visit our grandparents in Los Angeles. I remember how exciting those train trips were. One time our train came to a dead stop on a trestle over the Rio Grande: through the windows we looked down into the abyss. For a kid from the flatlands of Iowa, this was akin to landing on the moon. After we arrived in Los Angeles, of course, we were taken to the ocean, which was a very big deal.

At Christmas in Los Angeles, the weather was like summer in Iowa, where the tall corn grows. I remember being taken out by an uncle and looking through an orange grove to these snow-covered mountains. It was near Claremont. Maybe because of that, I later was persuaded to go to Pomona College, which was in a group of orange fields in the 1930s, long before Claremont became suburbanized. Not too far from my dormitory, I could look up through an orange grove similar to one I looked through as a young boy.

Sunset, March 1911.

These trips certainly helped indoctrinate my brother and me to the West at a very impressionable age. My father was way ahead of us, of course. He was thinking about our family's future in the West. His work at Meredith made him sensitive to just how important regional matters were to his readership. And of all the regions he covered, the Far West stood out more than any other, for its climate, its vegetation, and the special challenges and opportunities it offered.

These observations reinforced his growing certainty that this unique Western world was being inadequately served by Midwestern-based magazines and needed a voice of its own, a magazine devoted exclusively to the ways of Western living that were truly different from those east of the Rockies. Although he was aware that regional magazines had failed with dismal regularity in the past, he was certain that Western America offered all the necessary ingredients—socioeconomic, geographic, and cultural—to successfully support a regional publication.

It was on one of these California tours that my father came upon *Sunset*. Despite the booming economy of the 1920s, the magazine had fallen on hard times. Its glory days as an arm of the Southern Pacific were behind it. In 1914 S.P. had sold the magazine to a group of staff, who decided to try to turn it into a literary magazine of national significance, a kind of *Atlantic Monthly* of the West. The new owners believed that the time was ripe to publish a literary vehicle for the works of a flourishing crop of talented Western writers, poets, artists, and photographers. Jack London, who had first appeared in 1903 with his "Faith of Men," reappeared often over the years. Ambrose Bierce, Stewart Edward White, Joaquin Miller, William Rose Benét, George Sterling, Peter B. Kyne, Kathleen Norris, Erle Stanley Gardner, Aimee Semple McPherson, David Starr Jordan, Joseph Henry Jackson, Frank J. Taylor, and many other well-known authors and artists were featured on *Sunset* covers and in the pages of the magazine.

But the new owners sorely missed having a railroad bank account behind their worthy efforts, and the magazine had a financial statement tinged with red. *Sunset*'s hard luck turned out to be my father's good fortune.

By 1928 things were in transition at Meredith Publishing, and when Mr. Meredith died that year, his son-in-law, a very competent man named Fred Bowen, became president. This helped my father decide to go out on his own. He had had a very fine offer from the Curtis Publishing Company in Philadelphia, which was publishing *Saturday Evening Post*, the leading magazine at the time and a leader in the industry, and also *Ladies' Home*

Laurence and Ruth Lane with Bill and Mel in Iowa circa 1928, the year Laurence purchased *Sunset*, an anniversary marked in the pages of *Stet*, the *Sunset* staff newsletter, in October 1961.

CONGRATULATIONS, MR. LANE, ON YOUR 33rd YEAR!

A THIRD OF A CENTURY AGO . . . this family group had its picture taken in Des Moines, Iowa. Shortly afterwards, on October 12, 1928, Mr. Lane celebrated Columbus Day as he landed from the ferry in San Francisco to take over ownership of the struggling SUNSET Magazine. Mrs. Lane and the boys drove West just before Christmas. This Columbus Day Mr. Lane will celebrate his 33rd anniversary as "discoverer" of the Magazine of Western Living.

Journal. But *Sunset* was available for sale for what turned out to be $60,000, and Dad grabbed the opportunity. With the help of six other Des Moines investors, he purchased the magazine.

Dad immediately established a new program for *Sunset*. "The magazine," it declared, "will be maintained as a strictly western one, designed to serve western and national advertisers in reaching the substantial homes of the western states. Editorially, a large portion of the magazine will be devoted to the home and outdoor life of the west." *Sunset* was the clay, so to speak, that my father would now mold into something unique and quite different. But—and this is what many people overlook—he did so based to a large extent on his experience with Meredith.

Dad conceived of a magazine like *Successful Farming* that was devoted in a very vertical way to catering exclusively to families—as *Successful Farming* did in the Midwest—only now it was families living in the seven Western states. And he used the how-to-do-it, service-oriented editorial format of *Successful Farming*, a format aimed at both the man and the woman of the house. He also adopted from *Better Homes and Gardens* the editorial fields of food and garden and home. The new *Sunset* would expand on that formula by including articles on travel: from day hiking tours close to home to statewide and foreign trips.

An extremely important carryover from *Better Homes and Gardens* came in the form of two of its young associate editors, Lou Richardson and Genevieve Callahan. Dad asked them if they would go with him to be co-editors of the new *Sunset*. They eagerly signed on.

A letter my father wrote from San Francisco, dated October 28, 1928, to Lou and Gen in Des Moines shortly before they came west shows how intent he was on having *Sunset* target a particular audience. "Whatever the contents of Sunset Magazine may be," he wrote, "it must deal with life and conditions of life found west of the Great Divide and to a great extent must be confined to the three Pacific Coast states as it is there we find most of the population." His focus in 1928 was on the middle classes and the well-to-do residents of California, Washington, and Oregon. "Certainly in these states there is an abundance of money, motor cars, country homes and desire and ability to have the best of everything. Strange as it may seem with this condition we find among the people of the Coast a surprising spirit of friendliness and good fellowship with almost an utter lack of snobbishness. Certainly this is the thing to keep in mind in outlining the editorial program."

This uniquely unsnobbish Western personality, as Dad saw it, presented an opportunity to stretch for a substantial readership. He stressed that while the contents of the magazine should be aimed at families with no less than $5,000 income, it should not be afraid to address families enjoying income as high as $30,000. "The tone and physical appearance of the book should be comfortable, friendly, cheerful and smart without being 'smartty,'" he wrote to Lou and Gen. "I can't help but feel that we can make Sunset a 'mass' magazine in point of coverage and at the same time a 'class' magazine in point of editorial contents and appearance." And in fact this is exactly what Dad and his staff would achieve.

Larry Lane's arrival in San Francisco to take control of Sunset was auspicious. It was October 12, 1928. After crossing by boat from the end of the railroad at the Oakland Mole, he landed on the shores of the city, at the foot of Market Street. He was to be met there by the fellow he had hired to analyze Sunset's circulation, kind of a huckster but nonetheless a pretty nice guy. Anyway, this fellow came down to meet my father in a big open Cadillac.

As Dad stepped off the ferryboat, he was greeted by a brass band and an impressive parade. The fanfare, and the sight of that Cadillac, threw him for a loop. He had no way of knowing that the celebration in his midst was not a warm San Francisco welcome for the new publisher, but merely part of the Columbus Day festivities. Columbus Day was not a legal holiday or celebrated at all in Des Moines, Iowa, but it was a big deal in San Francisco, of course, with its significant Italian community.

It took my father a few minutes to get his bearings, and once he did, he saw the humor in it. In fact, he used to tell that story often. That symbolism always seemed apt to us. In making the move to California, Dad set the tone for our family to revere the excitement of discovery and to welcome the challenge of the future. That's the reason that Columbus Day was a holiday for all Sunset employees and, starting in the 1940s, that Sunset's longtime employees were called Columbians. You became a Columbian when you had served with the company for fifteen years.

Genevieve and Lou came out to San Francisco in November 1928 and got to work. My mother waited until Mel and I had finished school in December. Shortly before Christmas, we climbed aboard our new Packard—our covered wagon, you might say—and headed west. Dad's mother, Grandma Lane, came with us. Cecil, the caretaker on our Iowa farm, was our driver. We drove out with luggage stacked up on one running board above the side back window, on the trunk, and on a roof rack.

We spent that Christmas in Los Angeles with my grandmother Bell (my grandfather had passed away the year before) in her house off Wilshire Boulevard. Between Christmas and New Year's, we drove up Highway 1, along the coast, stopping at the Santa Maria Inn for one night, then coming into the Clift Hotel in San Francisco, near Union Square, on New Year's Day. We moved into a rented home on Adeline Drive in Burlingame, on the peninsula, about twenty miles south of San Francisco.

Despite all the excitement, my brother and I still missed our best friend back in Iowa—until one day, not long after we had gotten settled in, when my father returned from a business trip. I remember meeting him at the train, over at the Oakland Mole, the big barn where the transcontinental trains arrived and passengers could board the ferryboats to San Francisco. We always met him over there, and saw him off in San Francisco, where he took the ferry across to Oakland. On that day, Dad got off the train and said, "Wait a minute." He went back to a baggage car and brought out Cleta, our German shepherd, who had been cared for in Iowa after we moved west. That was a big day because we had hated to leave Cleta behind in Des Moines. With Cleta among us, our family was now complete.

Our *Sunset* Family

The first issue of the all-new *Sunset* appeared in February 1929. Dad had gotten the wheels turning before he actually took ownership in October of 1928. One of them was the plan for the first Lane cover, a beautiful oil painting of Emerald Bay, at Lake Tahoe. That cover was commissioned from Maurice Logan, whom Dad had met earlier on a trip out west.

The covers prior to February were quite different. Occasionally they portrayed home and travel, quite often just travel. I think Dad commissioned this one because it showed the home and the lake and the mountains, so it combined home and travel to set the new theme. In any case, that first Lane cover was memorable. I kept Maury Logan's original painting and hung it in my home.

Not that the earlier *Sunset* covers were not outstanding. "Taken cumulatively," in the words of historian Kevin Starr, "*Sunset* covers from the first four decades of the century yield some of the finest iconography and image-making dealing with Western life. Across scores of covers was achieved an almost utopian presentation of the landscape, people, and pleasures of the Far West."

So my father continued that venerable tradition. Certainly the cover of the February 1929 issue did not reveal the radical changes he had brought to *Sunset*. Open the pages of the magazine, however, and there could be no doubt that the maiden issue represented a completely new concept in magazine publishing. In one fell swoop it became a magazine for Westerners only, rather than one *about* the West for anyone living *any*place. Its pages spelled out the four major editorial fields to be covered in subsequent issues—home, garden, food, and travel—which would remain the magazine's principal concerns.

That first Lane issue had some holdover material from the old *Sunset*, but now the magazine featured how-to articles on travel, gardening,

Sunset, February 1929.

cooking, and home maintenance. A two-page spread in the first issue was called "Kitchen Cabinet," and presented recipes submitted by readers and tested in Mom's kitchen at home. "Kitchen Cabinet," always accompanied by how-to-do-it illustrations, would become a mainstay of Lane *Sunset*. As Kevin Starr wrote on the occasion of *Sunset*'s centennial in 1998: "Martha Stewart is a powerful figure in our culture. But she is just doing what *Sunset* began doing 70 years ago."

Overnight, *Sunset* went from being a literary magazine to being a how-to magazine. As my dad liked to say, "*Sunset* is not *about* the West; it's *for* the West." He changed the magazine's subtitle at first to "The Western Magazine of Homing and Roaming." He changed it several more times until, in 1943, he settled on "The Magazine of Western Living," and that one stuck.

As I've mentioned, Dad intended *Sunset* to appeal to the man of the household as well as the woman, and here's where the Martha Stewart analogy perhaps falls a bit short. In the West, as my father could see, a lot more of the living experience was shared by both the man and the woman. Men did more gardening, for one thing. Barbecuing was more popular in the West, and you could do it year-round. Dad saw this as an opportunity for *Sunset*, and it became part of the magazine's distinctive personality. There was some fine-tuning to be done in those first few years, but before long my father had redefined *Sunset* as the time of the late-afternoon commute, the time when one heard the call of home and sensed that *Sunset* meant home.

The fact that attention was paid to the man of the house is especially interesting when you consider the pioneering role of women in the early Lane *Sunset*. The top editorial responsibility fell to Lou as managing editor and Genevieve as home economics and food editor. (In the very first Lane issue, in February 1929, Laurence Lane appears on the masthead as managing editor, but he very quickly dropped that title.) The first travel editor was also a woman, Helga Iverson. These were unprecedented roles for women in the magazine industry. I daresay that *Sunset* may have been the first reputable magazine to have a female editor. And of course, off the masthead but absolutely crucial to the magazine's development was my mother, who was there to counsel my father, as well as give him encouragement.

The new *Sunset* could have turned out to be a short-lived experiment. Eight months after that inaugural Lane issue appeared, in October 1929, the stock market crashed, and before long the Great Depression set in. The pinch was felt pretty quickly in the *Sunset* offices. The Depression was hard enough on established firms, but for a new business nursing a sick property back to health, it was almost a death blow. But Dad and a loyal staff hung on.

Let's have a picnic!?

I'll make this Corn Tamale Pie in Sunset

Remove tamales from their husks ~

Add all other ingredients and mix well ~

An Invitation

WILL you share your favorite best recipes of all kinds with the other readers of Sunset, through the Kitchen Cabinet? This recipe exchange is a regular department, and $1 is paid for every recipe published. Address the Kitchen Cabinet, Sunset Magazine, 1045 Sansome Street, San Francisco.

The Kitchen

These recipes are designed to be clipped and mounted on cards for your recipe file, or they may be pasted in your cooking scrap book

Corn Tamale Pie

(For Your Next Picnic)

1 large can of golden bantam corn	1 small can of tomato sauce
1 large can of tamales	2 eggs, beaten
Salt and pepper to taste	

Mix corn, tamales, tomato sauce, and beaten eggs thoroughly together. Salt and pepper to taste. Butter an oven-ware or aluminum baking-dish and put the mixture into it. Bake in a moderate oven (375 degrees) for 30 or 40 minutes, or until the center of the tamale pie is firm. Grated cheese may be sprinkled over the top before baking for a more tasty crust.

To pack for the picnic, cover the tamale pie and wrap the baking-dish in several layers of newspaper. Place in a box separate from the rest of the picnic lunch. It may be reheated over the camp fire while the coffee is cooking if the trip is a long one.

With buttered rolls, celery or cold artichokes with mayonnaise, coffee, and dessert, this makes a simple and delicious picnic luncheon.—R. T. W., Berkeley, California.

Olive Oil Pickles

75 cucumbers (4-inch size)	1 tablespoonful of black mustard
½ cupful of salt	seed
1 pound of pickling onions	2 tablespoonfuls of celery seed
1 tablespoonful of white mustard	1½ cupfuls of salad oil
seed	4 cupfuls of vinegar

Wash the cucumbers carefully in cold water. Slice thin, without paring, sprinkle with the salt, and let stand in a crock overnight. Peel and slice the onions thin. Drain the cucumbers, mix with the sliced onions and the spices, and arrange in crocks or glass jars. Add the vinegar gradually to the oil, beat well, and pour over the pickles, mixing with a knife to allow the dressing to reach every part of the vegetables. If a crock is used, cover with a plate; if glass jars are used, screw on the lids, and keep in a cool place. I like best to store them in pint or half-pint jars.—Mrs. K. W., Hoquiam, Washington.

Grape Ham

When baking ham, cover the roast with a generous quantity of grapes, any kind, halved and seeded. Add 1 cupful of brown sugar and ½ cupful of white sugar for each 2 pounds of grapes. Cover and bake until done. Add no water after the grapes are put in. When done, remove the ham to a platter, thicken the juice in the pan with thin flour paste, and serve in a gravy boat.—Mrs. M. M., Long Beach, California.

Home-Canned Tomato Soup

14 quarts of ripe tomatoes, sliced but not peeled	14 tablespoonfuls (⅞ cupful) of butter
14 stalks of celery, chopped	14 tablespoonfuls (⅞ cupful) of flour
14 sprigs of parsley, minced	
7 medium-sized onions, sliced	8 tablespoonfuls of salt
14 bay leaves	6 tablespoonfuls of sugar
21 whole cloves	4 tablespoonfuls of paprika

Boil together, until tender and well-cooked, the tomatoes, celery, parsley, onions, bay leaves, and whole cloves. Let cool, run through a sieve, and heat again to boiling. Melt the butter, and add the dry ingredients; add two or three cupfuls of the hot soup and cook, stirring, just as you make white sauce. When smooth, stir this into the entire quantity of soup, let boil for a few minutes, and seal in sterilized glass jars. This recipe makes 12 to 14 pints of soup. It can, of course, be divided very easily. It may be used as it comes from the can, or thinned with water or milk. When milk is to be used, add a pinch of soda to the hot tomato mixture, and then stir it into the hot milk.—Mrs. P. B., Dilley, Oregon.

"The Kitchen Cabinet," from the July 1930 issue of *Sunset*.

Cabinet ~

A Real Pot-Roast

Rub the meat—preferably second-cut rump or sirloin tip—with salt and pepper; put into a kettle and pour boiling water over to sear it. Cover and cook slowly 2 or 3 hours, keeping the water about ⅛ the depth of the roast. When done, pour off liquid into a bowl; set the meat back on the fire and put in 4 or 5 tablespoonfuls of the liquid. Fry the roast in this until it crackles and sputters; turn over, put in a little more liquid, cover and fry again. Repeat this process until the roast has a rich brown crust all over it.

Put the roast on a platter in the warming oven while making the gravy. The liquid left in the kettle is mostly melted fat. Put into this a tablespoonful or two of flour, stir smooth, pour the rest of the liquid in, adding as much water as necessary, cook gently, and flavor to taste.

The flavor of the roast may be varied by cooking an onion with it, or a bit of lemon peel, or 2 or 3 cloves, or a bay leaf, or a spoonful of some of the prepared sauces. The gravy, too, is pricked up in accent by adding a cupful of chili sauce, or clear tomato sauce, or a bit of onion juice or onion or garlic salt. To flavor the roast and gravy adds piquancy to the dinner built up around them.—J. T., San Jose, California.

Raspberry Whip

1¼ cupfuls of crushed raspberries   White of 1 egg
1 cupful of powdered sugar

Put the ingredients into a large bowl and beat with a wire whisk until stiff (about 30 minutes or until it will hold its shape). Line a dish with ladyfingers and pile the mixture in lightly. Chill for an hour or two in the refrigerator. Serve with boiled custard or cream. By substituting strawberries, a delicious strawberry whip can be made by the above recipe.—Mrs. O. T. F., Bellingham, Washington.

Cooked Salad Dressing

¼ cupful of butter   1 tablespoonful of flour
2 egg yolks   1 tablespoonful of sugar
¼ cupful of vinegar   ⅛ teaspoonful of mustard
¾ cupful of boiling water   ½ teaspoonful of salt

Blend together the butter and the egg yolks. Place in a saucepan the vinegar and water, and thicken with the flour which has been mixed with the sugar, mustard, and salt. Cook, stirring, a few minutes, until smooth, then pour over the egg and butter mixture and beat thoroughly. Thin with plain or whipped cream as needed. Lemon juice may be used instead of the vinegar.—Mrs. E. W. R., Holley, Oregon.

Dried Beef a la Southern

2 tablespoonfuls of chopped onion   1 No. 2 can of corn
½ green pepper, chopped   2 tablespoonfuls of chopped
2 tablespoonfuls of butter   pimento
½ pound of dried beef   Salt and pepper

Brown the chopped onion and green pepper in the butter, then add the other ingredients, and simmer for 15 minutes. Served on toast or biscuits or in patty shells, this makes an interesting luncheon dish. —I. S., Pullman, Washington.

Spiced Green Peaches

7 pounds of green peaches (whole)   2 quarts of vinegar, diluted to
3 pounds of brown sugar   mildness
1 tablespoonful of whole cloves   1 teaspoonful of whole allspice
½ dozen 2-inch sticks of cinnamon

Tie the spices in a cheesecloth bag, and put with vinegar and sugar. Bring all to boiling, then add the peaches and cook until they are heated through. Pour all into a crock and let stand until next day. Drain off the juice, boil it for several minutes and pour over the peaches again. The third day, cook all together slowly until the peaches begin to soften, then dip out the peaches carefully, boil the syrup a little longer, pour over the fruit again, and put the bag of spices on top. Cover with a clean, wet cloth, then with paper, or put into glass jars and screw down the lids. They need not be sealed air tight.—Miss M. A. S., Oakland, California.

Put into oiled baking dish and bake until the center is firm—about 40 minutes. Cover and wrap hot dish in newspapers. Take on the picnic. Ruth Taylor White

An Announcement

THE special contests dealing with western-grown fruits and vegetables will be suspended for the space of a few months. On page 54 of this issue, however, you will find the announcement of a new and unusual competition open to all western homemakers. Please see page 54.

Hard times kept Dad very busy, and he was on the road a lot. Yet he managed to spend quality time with us boys. Between his long business trips to the East and the Midwest, he made time for camping and horseback riding. On Sundays we usually climbed into the car for a long drive somewhere. Often we were joined by Lou and Gen, who had become close friends of my parents' back in Iowa. In fact, we had purchased our pony, Betty, from a relative of Gen's. So all the Lanes were very close to them. In our big Packard we used to take day trips and even weekend trips to the wine country or up the Mendocino coast together. Lou and Gen were spinsters, and they lived together. They were just lovely women.

My fascination with aviation continued in California, for the first time as a passenger. Not long after we settled in Burlingame, Dad put Mel, Mom, and me in a privately piloted little single-engine plane. It had a hole in the floor, and I remember looking down at the San Francisco Bay as we took off. I don't recall any explanation for this opening, nor the reason why my father didn't come up with us. Maybe it had to do with weight capacity. Like a lot of these early memories, the context is lost, but looking down at the bay waters below, I may have wondered if Lindbergh had had a direct view of the Atlantic during his historic flight.

In 1930, Dad ran an early *Sunset* cover showing a different plane, a Ford Trimotor. It was a painting by Maynard Dixon, who designed some of the most memorable early *Sunset* covers. This one was a strikingly colorful blend of mountainous scenery, with a home along a river down below. I asked my father about the special appeal of that cover, and he explained that this plane was flying low, down amid the mountains: there could be no mistaking that this was in the West, because such high mountains didn't exist in any other part of the country. Later, when I was working in sales for *Sunset*, I took with me a reprint of that very fine 1930 cover as a kind of trademark of the magazine.

Sometime in the early 1930s my dad took us down to Moffett Field, a navy air base near Palo Alto, to see the two sister dirigibles the USS *Macon* and the USS *Akron*. At the time, they were the world's largest dirigibles, built by the Goodyear Company and only slightly smaller than the *Hindenburg*, which was built a few years later. I remember men pulling on ropes and slowly guiding one of these dirigibles into

Sunset, May 1930.

the post, leading it by the nose. The men let Mel and me hold the ends of the two ropes—a real thrill! The pilot would gun one motor, then another, and ease it down; then the men pulled the ropes and slowly got the point of the dirigible to hook up, then towed the aircraft inside that big hangar at Moffett Field.

Both of these dirigibles later crashed. The *Akron* crashed on April 4, 1933, in a storm off the coast of New Jersey, resulting in the deaths of seventy-eight people, including Rear Admiral William A. Moffett, whose name was then given to the navy base. Two years later, on February 12, 1935, the *Macon* met its end in a storm off Big Sur, killing two. The captain of the *Macon* escaped, and I was very happy for that: I was dating his daughter at Palo Alto High School! Still, it took the *Hindenburg* disaster in 1937 to bring the era of the dirigible to an end.

Bill and Mel, as they appeared on the Lane family's 1931 Christmas card.

In the 1930s Dad did much of his travel by train, and for years we used to drive over to the Oakland Mole to pick him up. Later, when the DC-3 came in, he started flying and we went to pick him up at Mills Field, which was located about where the United Airlines cargo hangar is today, near San Francisco Airport, along the old two-lane Bayshore Highway.

Being on the road a lot, Dad had little time for community activity. He had been a Mason in Iowa, but gave that up in California. For a time he was president of the San Francisco Kiwanis Club and served as president of the Advertising Association of the West. But he was enormously busy, because there was very little depth in the management of *Sunset*. It was a very hardy core of very committed people, and in the early Depression sometimes they couldn't even be paid. Still they remained loyal. That's where the term "*Sunset* family" originated.

There's no doubt that most of my father's energy and attention was devoted to the idea of making *Sunset* a success—and in the context of the Great Depression, that meant ensuring the magazine's very survival. He was often totally absorbed in the business. He didn't drink much in his early life, I don't think, but he sure enjoyed a martini or a scotch on the rocks. He was not a puritan, in the sense of holding rigid views of what made a good Christian. We never got lectures or preaching on morals that, say, a minister's son might recall (and a reason a lot of ministers' sons rebelled).

My brother and I never really had anything to rebel against, except I suppose if we had taken umbrage at the example that our family and relatives and friends set for us as we grew up.

My father was never a very religious person, but we boys did grow up in the Protestant church. In Des Moines, my grandmother was secretary of the church that we went to, which was part of Drake University. We went to Sunday school within a few blocks of where my grandmother lived. Later, in Burlingame, we went to Sunday school at the First Presbyterian Church, on the corner of Easton and El Camino Real.

I think as a family we were all committed to making *Sunset* successful, and we were made keenly aware of the seriousness of the Depression and the dire conditions that existed. If you look back at the early Lane *Sunset*, you see that the underlying editorial message has to do with courage and fortitude and looking on the bright side of things. In part this was because the times were so difficult. During the Depression you needed to keep moving forward, to put one foot in front of the other. But I think this was also the Lane philosophy, the way our family was raised. Over the years, in any activity I've been involved in with my children, I've heard them say, "Dad, you're always looking at the bright side," because I'm always saying that out of adversity almost inevitably comes opportunity.

My brother, Mel, and I grew up in the business, you could say. We worked in almost every department. One of the most valuable impressions I got as a kid during the Depression was selling *Sunset* door-to-door in Burlingame and learning how whole families used the magazine. Mel, two years younger, often joined me on my monthly rounds to offer the latest issue of *Sunset* to my "customers." We were part of *Sunset*'s very successful "Boy Sales" program. Whether it was my dad's intention or not, it was a subtle way to expose his sons to readers, giving us an opportunity to glean what men and women liked, and perhaps did not like, about *Sunset*.

I met readers early on Saturdays on these monthly calls. I saw husbands and wives both grabbing for the magazine. I saw firsthand, flesh and blood, how *Sunset* was a tool—not just a leisure pastime but a tool that was used to help these people in their lives. Later I added *Saturday Evening Post* and made weekly sales calls. This door-to-door selling was absolutely vital experience for me, and not just in my youth. Even as publisher I liked going out and meeting *Sunset* readers, to put my finger on the pulse, so to speak, of the magazine.

Mel and I did more than sell *Sunset* door-to-door. Through the later years of the Depression we worked Saturday mornings at the magazine's offices, which were open until one o'clock. The first office was on Sansome Street below Telegraph Hill above the Sunset Press, which was then no longer owned by Southern Pacific. I worked at the Sansome Street office sorting pied type, metal type characters dumped out after printing subscription letters. I sorted all those dinky little pieces of type back into their fonts.

I got paid for my work, although not very much. We always got a good lunch, though. In 1934, after *Sunset* moved from Sansome Street to 576 Sacramento Street—a slender seven-story tower building that still stands there—I continued working on Saturday mornings. When the office closed, we usually went across the street to a hamburger place for lunch. Occasionally we would get to go to Jack's restaurant, not far from *Sunset*, and that was a special treat.

The Sacramento Street building had a modest employees' cafeteria and they did a little testing there for the magazine. The test kitchen was another Meredith tradition. *Better Homes and Gardens* had test kitchens, and as I mentioned, my father was in charge of the cafeteria for employees at Meredith. But most of the testing for *Sunset* was done by my mother in her kitchen in Burlingame, and later in Palo Alto, and also in Lou and Genevieve's kitchen. Mel and I naturally became part of these culinary experiments, and not always willingly when it came to vegetable dishes, as I was later told. My mom once recalled that either Mel or I, on being asked whether his mother was a good cook, said, "Yes—when she's not testing those reader recipes." Mom also tried out many *Sunset* planting ideas in her garden in Burlingame and then in Palo Alto, where she was president of the Palo Alto Garden Club.

So the *Sunset* atmosphere in the Lane family was pervasive. But like most other kids, I was influenced by teachers and friends. I remember Mrs. Harris, who was my English teacher in grammar school—Roosevelt Grammar School, named after Theodore—my first school in Burlingame. I was nine years old at the time, and I recall her as a wonderful teacher. She would make us students close our eyes and tell us to envision a mountain stream, and the peace and quiet of a mountain valley, encouraging us to transcend our immediate environment and use our imaginations, stretch our minds. This was just after Byrd's exploration of the South Pole, which provided good inspirational material. As did, of course, the *Spirit of St. Louis*. "Picture yourself flying across the ocean," she would tell us. "Envision yourself in Antarctica."

I also remember Mr. Olsen, who was the principal at Roosevelt Grammar School, where Mom was president of the PTA. One time I was put out of a student body meeting because I whistled. Boy, did that make me mad. Then at one point I was elected student body president of my grammar school, so I got to know Mr. Olsen pretty well. Later in life, he and I became friends when he was made superintendent of the Menlo Park schools—after I had come down to Palo Alto High School. He was a wonderful man.

THIS Christmas number comes to you from a fine seven-story building at 576 Sacramento Street, in the heart of San Francisco's business district—in short, from SUNSET's new home.

Moving from the old quarters, long since inadequate, was accomplished just six years from the date when we set about to make of SUNSET a practical, interesting magazine devoted to western homes. It must be admitted that while our equipment was loaded into vans we indulged in just a bit of sentiment.

In those cramped old quarters had been crowded a lot of memories. There had been born our desire to supply the long-felt need of western families for information about western homes, western gardens and travel. And, although we recognized that improvement still is possible (and that we were moving to make it possible), we could not help rejoicing that the ever-widening approval of subscribers and advertisers had justified our past efforts.

This new home of SUNSET's, made possible by your loyalty and support, is designed to furnish you a better SUNSET. It is one of the finest publishing plants on the Pacific Coast, and every square foot of its space is devoted to one or another of the many operations necessary to the making of your SUNSET MAGAZINE.

On the first floor you will find the business offices and comfortable reception hall. Above this is the printing department where subscription notices, small circulars, and booklets are printed. The third floor is occupied by the

The
New Home
of
SUNSET MAGAZINE

A New Home That Means
A Better Western Magazine
For You To Use And Enjoy

❖

circulation department, where subscription records are kept. Offices of the advertising department occupy all of the fourth floor. The executive offices, together with the promotion and research departments, occupy the fifth floor. On the sixth floor you will find the editors and their assistants. The crowning glory of the building is the top floor, given over to our home economics department, our testing kitchen and dining room, a splendid working laboratory for SUNSET's department of western foods and their preparation. Here, too, is found a large recreation room and kitchenette for the use of employees.

The building will also enable us to render you a more complete service outside of the columns of SUNSET. Every year we have been glad to assist thousands of readers with advice on personal problems, and with improved facilities this service will be more valuable than ever before. A complete staff of consulting experts stands ready to assist you with detailed information in each of the subjects which SUNSET discusses editorially — in food preparation, building, home decorating, gardening, travel, and beauty.

We feel that we can be justly proud of this new home and that you can be proud with us. It is our hope that every one of SUNSET's more than 200,000 subscribers will at some time be able to visit this new home and inspect it from top to bottom. It was brought about through your cooperation; for you the latchstring always hangs out. Merry Christmas!—L. W. LANE, Publisher.

DECEMBER 1934

Drawing of the new *Sunset* headquarters at 576 Sacramento Street in San Francisco, from the December 1934 issue of the magazine.

We moved down to Palo Alto, to a rented house on Cowper Street, early in 1934. My brother went into grammar school in Palo Alto because he had more time to finish up. But I was close to finishing grammar school in Burlingame, so I commuted back and forth from Palo Alto to Burlingame on the train, all by myself. I remember that was quite a big deal. Then, in the fall of 1934, I started at Palo Alto High School.

In those early years we never could afford to buy a home or to build a home. We always rented. When there was a fire in our rented home on Cowper Street in Palo Alto in 1936, we moved a few blocks to an apartment on Forest Avenue. We were never an affluent family at all. We lived comfortably, but not at all high on the hog. In grammar school and then high school, I always had odd jobs going on in order to earn some spending money. I washed a lot of windows, I remember that. When I was in high school, I sold popcorn and programs at Stanford Stadium for the football games.

And of course I continued to help out at *Sunset*. My sense of commitment never flagged. I don't remember any pep talks from Dad or Mom, or some big crusade or lecture from them. We all knew what side our bread was buttered on and understood the necessity to make *Sunset* a success.

Sunset Gold

My father used to say—and I think this is important and I remind people of this—"Keeping a business alive, healthy, and growing, is harder than starting a business." You can debate the point, but starting a business is one thing, if you have analyzed the market, or if you're lucky or whatever and find a niche and find a path. But once your business is established, luck plays out pretty fast. You've got to be knowledgeable, you've got to be analytical, you have to be aggressive in the sense of boldness. And in fact the story of *Sunset*'s survival, let alone success, in the 1930s is not just one of optimism and fortitude, but also one of pioneering ideas.

First of all, the magazine's content was how-to-do-it, and usable information was especially valued during those Depression years. At the same time, *Sunset* held out before readers available opportunities to enjoy life in hard times. As Kevin Starr has so vividly described it, "Within the pages of the magazine there unfolded a panoramic pageant of gardening, architecture, regional cuisine, patio dining, golf, tennis, horseback riding, and other leisure pursuits, which represented, in its own way, a cunning strategy for economic success."

As early as September 1929, *Sunset* had experimented with a "Garden Guide" with different copy for three regions: northern, central, and southern. By 1932, it had become apparent to my father that as a regional magazine published exclusively for all Western families, *Sunset* was not hitting hard enough. The variations that made the West distinct from the rest of the country contained *internal* variables of their own. So, in the heart of the Depression, three separate sub-regional editions were created—Pacific Northwest, Central West, and Southern California—to reflect distinctions within the West caused by such differences in climate and environment that differentiate, say, Tacoma, Palo Alto, and Palm Springs. This was the first case of a consumer magazine "zoning" its contents in order to localize its editorial services.

My dad understood that he could use the regional editions to attract local business advertising, which could enter one of *Sunset*'s particular regions at a more affordable price. For many years *Sunset* carried far more regional advertising than any other magazine. Meanwhile, some of the major advertisers saw this zoning as an opportunity to try out different advertising copy in the three editions in order to determine what worked best.

Another pioneering technique was the use of department store charge accounts to pay for subscriptions. This enabled *Sunset* to obtain an automatic credit screening of our customers. For the stores, there was the advantage of helping to provide their preferred customers with a source of information and service that involved many of the products available at their counters. For the customers, the advantage was the convenience of being able to charge a subscription. We were one of only a handful of consumer publications that had a completely cash-in-advance operation. And circulation was strictly voluntary: there were no special offers, no premium sales, not on new sales or on renewals.

All of these techniques worked, and circulation figures rose steadily, surpassing 200,000 in 1932. The original *Sunset* had been a founder of the Audit Bureau of Circulation in 1913, but it had subsequently gotten off track on the quality of its circulation, and so it had lost the bureau's seal of approval. It had been using all kinds of handouts and gimmicks, so it was impossible to determine the number of verified paid subscriptions. My father was intent on getting the magazine back into the good graces of the Audit Bureau of Circulation, and in order to do so he had to get the "water" out of the circulation, so to speak. And he succeeded. By 1932, the quantity and quality of circulation again met the test of the Audit Bureau of Circulation, and *Sunset*'s charter membership was reinstated.

So there was no shortage of ideas behind Lane *Sunset*. Still, from a financial standpoint, Dad needed help, and he got it. Several families in Des Moines invested at the start, but bankruptcies washed out some of that early investment. The magazine underwent three reincorporations between 1928 and late 1933, each new corporation assuming the assets and liabilities of its predecessor. Together these corporations supplied total working capital of just under $1 million, all of it needed just to keep the magazine afloat. *Sunset* had generous credit from both the magazine's printer, Sunset Press, and its paper supplier, Crown-Zellerbach, to keep the magazine from sinking. It would be hard to exaggerate the importance of Crown-Zellerbach's contribution.

For several years *Sunset* could not always pay the bill for its paper. Isadore Zellerbach was very fond of Dad, very supportive, and he would advance the credit. Eventually, however, the debt got a little heavy, so at the beginning of 1934, he and Dad agreed that an outside individual should come in and evaluate *Sunset* and its potential future. That individual was James Webb Young, former executive with the J. Walter Thompson advertising agency and at that time professor of business history and advertising at the University of Chicago, a man highly respected within the magazine industry.

Mr. Young interviewed my dad and the key staff, pored over the books, and looked into every aspect of the business thoroughly. He came to the conclusion that the business was sound and promising. In fact, Mr. Young became so enthusiastic about it that he invested a sizable amount of his own money to keep the magazine going. Not only did he become an investor; he took control of *Sunset* in stock ownership, and he joined the board of directors.

It wasn't until the late 1940s or early 1950s that Mr. Young was paid off on a formula for his stock. Although for a period of time my father did not have the controlling ownership of *Sunset*, under the agreement he worked out with Mr. Young, Dad was to be the chief executive officer. And Mr. Young was a very considerate angel who never disputed Dad's leadership, because his sole interest was really to help him stay in business. We all got to know Mr. Young very well. He became a close family friend, and we all were aware of what he was doing to try to help us.

Mr. Young had two sons, and they also influenced the development of *Sunset*. One was a trader of Native American goods, especially weaving— Navajo blankets, Navajo woven ties, and various other Navajo products— based in Albuquerque, New Mexico, whose company was called Webb Young Trader. Mr. Young did copy testing of advertising for his son's business in *Sunset* using the three editorial editions. In the process, he helped perfect the regional editions of *Sunset*. Mr. Young had another son, who worked at the magazine, and that son helped perfect the staff writing technique of *Sunset*. This was yet another pioneering idea that my father introduced.

The idea to transition to an entirely staff-written magazine originated in 1935, when my father arranged a survey of readers and discovered that they favored shorter articles, in part because they could retain more of the content of shorter pieces. Dad decided, after some experimentation, that all articles in the magazine could be shortened considerably, most by up to one-third, without loss of essential content and without making them unfriendly or too blunt, and that the job could be done best by *Sunset*'s own editors.

So in February 1936 *Sunset* became the only entirely staff-written magazine aside from the major newsweeklies. This appealed to Dad, who not only was a man of few words but hated verbosity. It also appealed to Mom, whose father had authored a book on orthography in 1911 and who herself was a strong advocate of no-nonsense writing and editorial clarity.

There was another motive behind the move to staff writing. My father reasoned that if the name of an author appeared, a reader held him responsible for the article's accuracy. But if there was no byline, *Sunset* would be held responsible. *Sunset* would in every case be the real author. This would also help ensure that every effort would be made to make certain that *Sunset* could stand behind the accuracy and the authenticity of what appeared in the magazine.

By 1936, all the pieces of Sunset's distinctive personality were in place. In 1938, *Sunset* finally turned a profit. Its operating profit that year was $25,000, compared to a loss of $71,822 during the first year of Lane *Sunset*. In the Depression this was news, and *Time* magazine took notice with a special feature titled "Sunset Gold."

Buckaroo Bill

Getting experience and seeing for yourself—that was the *Sunset* ethos. Naturally, that way of thinking rubbed off on me. I even got personally involved in a small way during my student years, when Helga Iverson, the travel editor, got me a job on a freighter from Los Angeles to San Francisco. Helga was going to take the trip herself, but she had to change her plans at the last minute and she asked me to take her place. I traveled on a freighter that carried twelve passengers up and down the coast. I guess that was my first scouting assignment. I believe I was at Stanford, but I'm not sure what year it was. Although I'm vague on the details, the thinking behind it was quintessentially *Sunset*: see for yourself.

Helga had taken pack trips in the mountains with Norman B. "Ike" Livermore, Jr., who was very active in organizing the packers in the High Sierras. She had interviewed the packers and the pack station staff, and she wrote about it for *Sunset*.

Ike was someone who had an early influence on me. In the summer of 1934, Dad took Mel and me on a pack trip out of Mineral King, with the Mineral King Packing Company, in Sequoia National Forest. Ike packed us

PHOTO BY PRASHERS'

PHOTO BY LAVAL CO., INC.

Mountains and Meadows Invite
You to the Heart of the Sierra

Take a
Pack Train
to Paradise

Urges

Claude M. Kreider

T HERE is a peculiar charm about horseback and pack train travel in high mountain country, which is foreign to the usual variety of summer vacation trip. Especially will you know this indefinable appeal when you bestride a good mountain horse and start your pack outfit into the tremendously rugged California Sierra. You realize, with a thrill, that you are independent of civilization for a week, or a month; that you are about to prove to your own satisfaction that you can live comfortably, and joyously, by your own efforts.

The pack animals carry your food, bed, and simple equipment which, if properly chosen, will provide all the necessary comforts, and a few simple luxuries such as an air mattress, folding reflector baker, a light waterproof tent, or half a case of eggs. You make camp where you choose, and at any time you like. Within an hour after this decision, a meal may be ready, the beds laid out, and the animals hobbled in the rich meadow grass. Then you may fish for trout, hunt deer, gather in small game for the pot, or simply rest.

Here let me urge the uninitiated who have never gone beyond a road end, and who hazily wonder how to go about it, that a pack trip is feasible and practicable for them, granting careful planning in advance and a fair sprinkling of common sense on the trail.

Those who like to stroll along mountain trails, who can do eight or ten miles a day without excessive fatigue, and who have sufficient time for a leisurely trip, may choose burros for their pack animals, with assurance of a mini-

mum of trouble with these faithful and intelligent little beasts. They will care well for your packs, because they value their own precious skins very highly. Also, they may be rented from outfitters at almost any point along the Sierra foothills at an astonishingly low rate. A burro will carry 125 pounds with ease. Thus, one to each member of the party will be ample for a trip up to three weeks

A page from the July 1930 issue of *Sunset*.

for that trip, and by the time it was over, I knew that packing mules was something I would like to do.

The next summer I applied for a job with Phil Buckman. The Buckman family owned the Mineral King Packing Company. Buckman gave me what in Australia you would call a buckaroo job, just a handyman to do whatever was needed. It was the lowest-grade job, paying $15 a month and "found"—meaning a bed and food. The bed was an old cot under a tree and the food was mostly milk and peanut butter sandwiches, as I recall. That first summer, when I was in Palo Alto High School and I was fifteen years old, I shod horses and mules. I'd already been around horses a lot as a boy.

At that time Mineral King was in the Sequoia National Forest, and not yet a part of the national park. There was a big fish-breeding operation, a fish farm there for the U.S. Forest Service. I was loaned to both of the pack companies there. Of course the packers wanted the lakes that they packed people in to have a supply of fish. So when there was a lull in business they would loan mules and a packer and a horse to take these fish in.

A good part of my work was planting virgin lakes around Mount Whitney. You had to go across the Kern-Kaweah basin, the big drainage from the High Sierras to Southern California that comes out at Bakersfield—there's great river running down at that lower end—so it was a two- or three-day trip. The lakes would have an inlet where these fish, which were really minnows, could later breed.

The fish were carried in what we called milk cans, and in fact some of them actually were milk cans. They were strapped on with the handles, and they had a screened top. If the lake was more than one day's ride away, you had to aerate the fish all the way in and keep them aerated. This was more involved than it might at first sound.

The pack train usually had eight mules that were head-to-tailed, which means that the lead rope was tied onto the tail of the mule ahead. I lost a mule once, and it had an influence on me for the rest of my life. As I say, the water for these fish had to be aerated all the time. At night you took the cans off and put them in the stream, with the wire mesh facing upstream so that they were getting fresh water. Then when loading them in the morning, you had to walk down the line and continually rock them as you loaded up one and then another. When you got on the trail, of course, they aerated themselves, but on an incline you had to rest your animals.

Whenever you stopped, you had to walk up and down and rock the cans, and a lot of times you were on very narrow trails. It could be dangerous, and occasionally a mule would slip and you might lose a mule. That's exactly what happened to me. It was a very reliable mule who would follow the string, so I had let her go alone at the end of the string—in other words, I had not head-to-tailed her. She was carrying all of my personal gear and food. Well, she slipped off and flipped and rolled into a stream. I got her out and she was all right, but my bedroll was soaked and all of my food was gone.

All I had in my saddlebag was a couple of boxes of raisins, so I lived on raisins and water for the rest of that trip. It was only two or three days, but that experience gave me a strong bias against raisins. I just wouldn't eat raisins. Anyway, that's my fish story. My wife, Jean, and the kids have heard it a thousand times.

That was the summer that Will Rogers died, in August 1935. I had listened to Will Rogers a lot on the radio as a kid. And my father had liked him, and I think maybe had met him. So it hit me hard when, during one of my packing trips, a ranger came through on the Muir Trail and said, "Will Rogers was killed in a plane crash in Alaska." I had a little campfire there and I was all alone, and I remember I sat and cried. The moment has never left me.

One of my assignments that summer was to pack mining equipment in to a mine, which was permitted then in the national forest. It wouldn't be today, because that little pocket in the southern end of Sequoia is now part of the national park, but there was a mine moving in, and we had to come up with an ingenious way to take a cable for a bridge. We figured out we could loop the cable around three or four mules, and then loop it back on the other side. It was a very precarious way to pack this cable in. I finally got it packed in up into this canyon, but I remember at the time I was not at all sympathetic to the idea of mining in that beautiful setting. I probably wasn't aware of the pollution hazards for the water, but it just seemed incompatible to me for what was obviously going to be a very marginal mining operation.

Anyway, that summer of 1935 I did some packing as a junior packer, working for Ike Livermore. On one occasion we picked up a party—a "dude trip," it was called—and brought them from Sequoia all the way into Yosemite. At the end of that trip they asked me if I'd like to pack out of Yosemite the following summer. I said yes, and the following summer I began packing supplies into the Yosemite Park and Curry Company's "High Sierra Camps."

I returned to Yosemite and worked the summer of 1938, after graduating from high school. I did a lot of drudge work for Yosemite Park and Curry Company. At that time the company was still owned by the Curry family, and I went up there and worked at the stables. I also packed supplies into the High Sierra camps, and I was the buckaroo on the children's burro picnic.

Occasionally I would take rides out, guided rides into the valley, but mostly I was the junior man at the stable—which inevitably involved shoveling manure. I was definitely the low man on the totem pole. I got paid

$35 a month plus room and board. The board was canned baked beans and plain white bread and milk. The room was an open platform with a cot and a bedroll, and that was it.

I paid for my first radio and for my first car out of the money I earned from working in the mountains. I bought this little Model A Ford between my sophomore and junior years in high school. That car was my pride and joy: dark green, black fenders, a cabriolet roof, and a rumble seat. In 1937 my parents bought Quail Hollow Ranch, on three hundred acres in the Santa Cruz Mountains. I liked to drive the Model A to Quail Hollow on weekends and holidays, and I often brought along friends for a visit. Later I had a fraternity party or two at the ranch.

Quail Hollow Ranch is named for the valley in which it was located. My parents were able to purchase the ranch for very little money, on account of the Depression. They began a routine that brought them to the ranch for part of every week. For Mel and me, the ranch was a joy. It gave us unlimited opportunities for horseback riding, along what I christened the "Sunset Trail" around the property. Quail Hollow had a sizable orchard planted by the previous owners, and Mel and I discovered that the apples could fetch a handsome price in nearby Santa Cruz. We kept a cow on the ranch, and not surprisingly the milking chores often fell to me. Mel had ample opportunity to hone his considerable skill as a barbecue chef.

In 1938, the year when *Sunset* turned a profit, I graduated from Palo Alto High School and started at Pomona College. Pomona seemed like a natural choice for me. I liked Southern California. Looking at snow-covered mountains through orange groves when we came out from Iowa at Christmas was an enduring boyhood memory. We had a couple of good friends who had gone to Pomona College. Also, the school's recruiter gave a great pitch at Palo Alto High School. I loved Pomona. Mel also enrolled there, two years later. The only traumatic thing about it is that I had to sell my Model A Ford, because Pomona didn't permit freshmen to have automobiles.

Pomona was very strong in music, very strong in drama. That was another reason I chose it: I had been very active in debate and in acting at Palo Alto High School. Robert Taylor, the movie star, was an alumnus of Pomona, and he came and spoke to our drama class. My instructor, who later came to Stanford to teach drama, suggested to Taylor that a screen test be arranged for me in Hollywood, but by that time I'd convinced myself that I wanted to become part of *Sunset* after college.

Once I had made up my mind, I decided to transfer to Stanford for the start of my junior year. I wanted to study journalism, and Stanford had a very strong program. Chilton "Chick" Bush was the dean of the journalism school. He had come to Stanford from Wisconsin in 1934 and built journalism at Stanford into a formidable academic field. He was a former newspaper editor, and I remember that the program involved a great deal of writing under deadline. The thesis I wrote for my journalism major, titled "Germany and the Nazi Press," traced the rapid subjugation of a relatively open press in Germany as Hitler stormed to power and then consolidated his dictatorship, all with the help of his propaganda chief, Joseph Goebbels.

I became business manager of the student humor magazine, *Chaparral*, starting in my junior year, the first-ever junior to hold this position. At one point, *Chaparral* had been kicked off campus for its risqué humor—although by today's standards the jokes were rather tame. So I took a survey of students of the fraternity and sorority houses on campus. I was Delta Tau Delta myself. I just went around and talked to the students, the gals especially, about *Chaparral*, what they thought of the magazine. I discovered that few of them responded to those risqué jokes. They preferred the general articles and the sports. I convinced the editor that we could sell more copies—and be allowed to remain on campus—if we dropped some of the more provocative humor. After we did, we not only avoided being kicked off campus again, but I was able to attract more advertising for the magazine, enabling us to make a profit. It probably didn't hurt matters that I introduced a beauty contest, "Queen of the Month," and that we even had a bathing suit issue.

By the end of my junior year, in the summer of 1941, I began to wonder whether the draft might interrupt my senior year. The war in Europe had been under way for nearly two years, and Nazi Germany invaded the Soviet Union in June 1941. Tensions with Japan were rising, and it was unclear how long the United States could remain neutral. My dad was very supportive of the military and always valued his military training. He had encouraged me to go into the ROTC when I was at Pomona College, and he was very helpful in my getting into officer training at Stanford after my transfer.

After all the buildup, America's entry into the war did not come as a surprise, but the event that triggered it caused a tremendous shock. On Sunday, December 7, 1941, at around midday, I was driving near the Stanford campus when I heard the news over the car radio: Japan had launched a devastating attack on Pearl Harbor. I was about to answer a different kind of call to Go West.

Bill Lane as an ensign in the U.S. Navy, 1944.

Chapter 2

The Masthead

Officer

The war was a maturing experience for young men like me. After Pearl Harbor, Stanford president Ray Lyman Wilbur gave me a letter that the San Francisco navy recruiting officer accepted as a university degree. I had my officer training at Harvard University, and my first assignment for the navy was at the Monterey Naval Section Base, where I was on coastal patrol for Japanese submarines.

I was then assigned to the navy's public relations office, in the Federal Building in San Francisco. We worked very closely with the office of the commandant of the Twelfth Naval District, Admiral Carleton Wright. Admiral Wright had been demoted after committing a blunder in the Battle of Tassafaronga, in November 1942, during the Guadalcanal campaign. As a result, he had been beached and he was certainly not happy about that. One day he called me up and said, "Lane, I want you to be my aide and flag lieutenant." I said fine, I'd be proud to be.

So I became aide to Admiral Wright and was sent to Treasure Island as a public relations officer with the rank of ensign. Admiral Wright was an old sourdough dog who would have preferred to be out at sea, but he and I just hit it off. He adopted me as his son, and we became close friends. Among my other duties, I helped edit the weekly paper of the U.S. Naval Training Center, the *Masthead*. Mostly I stayed behind the scenes of the paper, but I did make an appearance in print in a New Year's editorial, dated January 1, 1944. It captures a sense of the moment, two years into America's involvement in the war. "We are unlocking the door to the third New Year since this World War II began for the United States," I began.

> This year will be a crucial year. It will be a fatal year or a successful year. In no sense will it, or should it, be a totally Happy Year. It will be a year of sorrow, bloodshed, unbelievable sacrifice of energy and time, and a

deep and profound determination to do more than our share. There can be only one result . . . a group of independent nations that has whipped a couple of bullies and can go back to living in a world of peace.

During the San Francisco World's Fair of 1939, the alcove on Treasure Island had been used for the Pan American Clippers flying in and out, a service that Pan Am had just begun. But during the war the navy took it over and began flying those Clipper planes. Admiral Wright functioned for a period as liaison with Admiral Chester Nimitz, commander in chief of the U.S. Pacific Fleet, based in Hawaii, and one time he asked me to deliver a personal message from him to Admiral Nimitz. So I flew to Hawaii, and as the junior man on the plane I was bounced to the back of the aircraft, where sacks of mail served as my bed during the eight-hour flight.

When I introduced myself to Admiral Nimitz, he said to me, "Lane? Is that *Sunset* magazine? My wife and I are rosarians"—meaning they cultivated roses. And in fact, outside his office at the army base at Pearl Harbor, and later on Guam, he had a little rose garden. After the war, Nimitz and his wife visited *Sunset* headquarters in Menlo Park. He became quite a fine gardener, and after he retired and lived on Claremont Avenue in Berkeley he won prizes for his rose gardens.

Early in 1944 I requested sea duty and was assigned to a troop transport. My ship was the *Moore McDove*, a Moore McCormick freighter that had been converted to a troop transport. All these freighters were named for birds—*Moore McSwan*, *Moore McGull*, *Moore McThis*, *Moore McThat*. The merchant marine was brought into the navy, and we had gun and communications crews. That was the way I spent most of the last two years of the war: as a gunnery officer on a navy troopship in the Pacific. I started a radio broadcast on the ship. We usually had some entertainers among the troops, so we had tryouts for our daily program of singing and short skits.

The war matured you quickly. On my ship I managed about fifty or sixty gunners, and I had about thirty in communications. It was a good lesson in being given responsibilities and being held accountable. That level of responsibility was not unusual for a person in his mid-twenties in wartime. By the time I got my troopship I was a lieutenant JG (junior grade), and later a full lieutenant.

My brother, Mel, had a similar wartime experience. Like me, he received his naval officer training at Harvard University. Mel had been admitted to the Marine air corps, but he punctured an eardrum, so I helped him get into the navy in the supply corps. He was made a supply officer on a destroyer, also patrolling in the Pacific. Our ships were generally used in convoys for protection against Japanese submarines. Mel's ship was out at sea when he graduated from Stanford, in June 1944, and I remember my ship was in, so I went with my parents to his graduation. They awarded him his degree because he had completed all of his credits from Stanford.

Over the years Mel and I put a high priority on our similar military service for influencing our discipline and our respect for each other. In August 1945, when I was in the Lingayen Gulf waiting with a load of marines to go on an invasion of Japan, the war ended with the atom bomb. I didn't know it at the time, but my brother had been involved in the Battle of Okinawa on a destroyer.

When the war ended, Admiral Wright asked me to come back and work for him, so I became his aide again, from October 1945 until February 1946. I was given an important and delicate diplomatic assignment. I came back to get Admiral Wright squared away with the local community, because the navy had gotten a terrible bashing in the press. Admiral Wright, being an old battleship admiral and knowing what it meant to have leave when a sailor got ashore, was the only military commander who gave liberty on V-J Day: the army and the air force didn't give liberty. So the navy men were all by themselves in tearing up the town, breaking windows and turning over streetcars and causing all kinds of mayhem. Admiral Wright got all hell blasted out of him by the press and the business community, and also by Fleet Admiral Ernest King, the navy's second most senior officer.

I worked for about four months to get the navy back in the good graces of the local politicians and merchants and the press. I never tried to rely on personality, but always tried to marshal the facts. I remember working up a presentation. I called on Ned Lipman, president of the Emporium, because all the store's windows had been broken by the sailors and the company was raising hell with the navy. I said to Mr. Lipman, "Those kids, a lot of them have gone through all kinds of battles, they won freedom here which you're going to benefit from. And just because you lost a few broken windows . . ." I'm paraphrasing now, but I had my line of argument all worked out ahead of time. My central point was that the decision of one man should not prejudice the entire press, let alone the owner of the Emporium, against the U.S. Navy.

I said to Mr. Lipman something like, "Can you tell me that in your business career you never made a decision on impulse that you didn't regret afterwards?" This was kind of presumptuous, I realized. He was amused and said, "That's a pretty cocky question for a young guy like you to be asking me"—something to that effect. We laughed about it afterwards. I said, "Admiral Wright was thinking of these boys who had earned this peace. None of your merchants put their lives on the line, but now they will benefit from the peace." Ultimately, we got the situation turned around.

Admiral Wright was the most un-*Sunset* person you could imagine, but his wife loved the magazine. When I was with him, before I went to sea, they created another command over him, Western Sea Frontier, and as a result they took his quarters on Yerba Buena island and gave it to Admiral J. W. Greenslade, a senior admiral who had been called out of retirement to command the whole seacoast plus Hawaii. So Admiral Wright was kicked out of his home, which usually was reserved for the commander of the Twelfth Naval District, and he was hopping mad about it.

I said to him, "Admiral, why don't we see if we can create a *Sunset* house." I knew his wife loved *Sunset*, and he was impressed that Admiral Nimitz was a great reader of *Sunset*, and he agreed. We got two chief's quarters and put them together. They had a view overlooking Treasure Island, a much better view than the other house, which looked out over the Oakland shipyard. I got one of our *Sunset* editors to give some advice, and he enlisted an architect to contribute a design for combining these chief's quarters and putting a shake roof over the new structure. The admiral moved in, and his wife was happier than a clam. She had a beautiful garden, and they had a beautiful view of the old World's Fair site on Treasure Island.

I continued doing this press relations job into 1946, but I was eager to get started at *Sunset*, and I had the points to get out of the navy. Actually, I had had enough points at the end of the war, but Admiral Wright convinced me that I should continue to serve my country. Mel and I both extended our military service: Mel's destroyer stayed at sea to participate in the Bikini atom bomb tests.

One day Admiral Wright called me in and he said, "Bill, I appreciate what you've done in getting our public relations back on track, and now I think it's time for you to go into your family business." By that time he had met my mother and father and had visited *Sunset*'s offices. So in February I left the navy and went to work at *Sunset*, starting out as elevator operator in the seven-story headquarters building at 576 Sacramento Street. I was starting at the bottom, but my sights were set on the top.

Apprentice

During the war, while my father remained active and very influential in the business, my mother served as managing editor of *Sunset*, a position she continued to hold into 1948. Mom was perfectly suited to the task. During her college years at Drake University she was assistant editor of the student newspaper, *Quax*, and a member of the Drake Literary Society. She would later become vice president of *Sunset*, and eventually would chair the Lane Publishing Company.

Both Mel and I came into *Sunset* in the same year, 1946. Dad and Mom started us out on a track that neither of us recognized at the time. Aside from my duties as elevator boy, I worked in the circulation department, writing circulation subscription letters. I had been a journalism major and I liked to write. I did some other odd jobs in the circulation department, just as Mel also took on lower-level jobs in other departments. Our assumption was that we would work our way up through the company. One day, however, Mom and Dad confronted us brothers directly.

We met up at my parents' apartment at the Mark Hopkins Hotel. In the late 1930s, my parents took ownership of this small apartment in place of a due bill for advertising by the hotel published in *Sunset*. They lived in the apartment, although during the war they spent a lot of time at their ranch, Quail Hollow, in the Santa Cruz Mountains. It was at this apartment in the Mark Hopkins that my parents really put it to us.

Mel and I talked about this encounter over the years, and we could never figure out for sure whether our parents were seriously tempted or were just testing our commitment. They were getting attractive offers from would-be buyers of *Sunset*. Dad had been approached by several friends in the business, among them Gardner "Mike" Cowles, Jr., *Look* magazine's co-founder and first editor, who was executive editor of the *Des Moines Register* and the *Des Moines Tribune*. I don't know if Henry Luce had contacted Dad or not, but DeWitt Wallace, a Minnesotan who co-founded *Reader's Digest* in 1922, at one time expressed a great deal of interest in acquiring *Sunset*.

Dad asked us boys straight out whether we really were planning to stay with the magazine or whether we wanted to change our careers. As I say, we weren't entirely sure how serious he was about selling, but we responded with an emphatic "Don't sell!" Morris Doyle, of McCutchen, Doyle, Brown & Enersen, the *Sunset* attorney, referred to this episode as Bloody Thursday, the day when Dad really put us on the spot.

Dad may not have been intent on selling the magazine, but now, in his mid-fifties, he definitely wanted to phase out, and during the war he had begun planning ahead. He hired Howard Willoughby, of the advertising firm Foster & Kleiser, to join *Sunset* as vice president, director, and general manager—"in case something happens to me" was how

Sunset, April 1946.

The higher the cost of walled-in rooms, the more your appreciation grows for open, usable outdoor "rooms" in which to play, loaf, and dine. A patio barbecue like the one in the garden of Mr. and Mrs. Donald Coen of Pacific Palisades, California, would be attractive in your garden even without a backdrop of the Pacific Ocean my father put it. Mr. Willoughby had been a friend of the family since the 1920s, a wonderful man. I remember coming to the office once during the war, when my ship came in, and learning that he had been hired, and I thought it was great.

Mr. Willoughby was very active in Alpha Delta Sigma, which was an advertising fraternity when I was at Stanford. He was certainly recognized as one of the real deans of the advertising industry, definitely here in the West. He functioned as chief operating officer of the magazine, under the strict guidelines of the policy book written by my dad. Now, beginning in 1946, his duties would also include supervising my brother's and my apprenticeships in the magazine business. That was Howard Willoughby's charge, and both Mel and I feel that he carried it out beautifully. His guidance was crucial to preparing us to run *Sunset*.

Mel and I took over an apartment in San Francisco, on Jones and Sacramento, which my parents had had to move into when the navy appropriated their floor at the Mark Hopkins in order to house returning flag officers. When the war ended and they moved back into their apartment at the Mark Hopkins, Mel and I moved into the Jones and Sacramento apartment. And we both just worked our tails off.

Dad made certain that our early training jobs sent a signal to the staff that "the Lane boys," as we were called, did *not* have silver spoons in their mouths. He told me later—and several other people in the business told me as well—that Mel and I came along much faster than he had anticipated. It helped that we were both bachelors, because the work was all-consuming. The company was small enough that the two of us moved through the business, doing rather menial chores always at the beginning of our tour, learning all aspects firsthand, but very soon taking on increasing responsibility.

In San Francisco for a few months we worked together managing *Sunset*'s book department. *Sunset*'s books started out in the early 1930s as mere pamphlets. One of the first little cook booklets we had was the *Grubstake Cookbook*, which I could relate to, because when I was a packer I used to cook in a reflector oven and a Dutch oven, which we'd bury in hot coals. The *Grubstake Cookbook* told you how to do it. The pamphlets were drawn largely from *Sunset* magazine copy. At first they were given away to the department-store charge-account customers who bought new *Sunset* subscriptions. But we found the department stores often asking for more of these pamphlets so they could sell them separately. So the pamphlets graduated to books, and we published nineteen titles before the war.

During the war a major problem, for both the books and the magazine, was the shortage of paper. Yet the War Ration Board allowed *Sunset* extra paper for its *Sunset Vegetable Garden Book* (1943), which promoted victory gardens. In 1946 came the first hardcover, large-format *Sunset* book, *Western Ranch Houses*, by *Sunset* editors and architect Cliff May. It was not long after the appearance of that book that Mel and I went into what was then the book department and ran a two-man band. The net result was that we proved to ourselves that book publishing was an activity that made a great contribution to the company, and in a very strong reciprocal relationship with the magazine. We had about ten titles in print at that time, and I was in charge of sales and editorial, while Mel handled production and business operations. Already the division of duties between us, the product of our different individual talents and interests, was apparent.

Rather than working entirely through our sales reps, I went out selling books myself. We bought an old secondhand Plymouth sedan, and I loaded up the backseat and the trunk and sold bookstore-to-bookstore, traveling all over the West. I made some wonderful friends of newsstand wholesalers who sold books on their newsstands and through the bookstores. These people would invite me into their homes and feed me and even house me sometimes. Those were great days. I still go through small towns, like Salem and Eugene, and remember when I used to call on the college bookstores. I did it all over the seven states where *Sunset* was primarily involved at the time.

My father had considered selling *Sunset* Books, but Mel and I convinced him that it was a winner. In 1949 Lane Publishing set up a separate book division that would extend the magazine's editorial service to a much larger audience and eventually sell several million books a year. By the late 1960s, after Mel had become publisher of *Sunset* Books, it was selling upwards of 1.5 million copies per year, which amounted to more than $50 million, with nearly half the sales outside the West. By the 1980s *Sunset* Books was offering hundreds of titles, many in multiple editions, packed with expert advice, much of it drawn from the magazine. Of all the *Sunset* books published over the decades, the most popular and the biggest seller by far was the *Sunset Western Garden Book*. (It had been preceded, in 1939, by *The Complete Garden Book*.) First published in 1954 and then frequently updated, it became the best-selling book in the West—not counting the Bible and the dictionary.

I remember my dad telling me, "You should work to be the best salesman in the company." And in fact, in my three sales assignments I did become *Sunset*'s highest-volume salesman. I started out as marketing rep—in fact, I was the very first *Sunset* marketing rep, appointed by my dad and Howard Willoughby.

The job of the marketing rep was to work with wholesalers and dealers on the West Coast. We would support any Eastern advertiser in their marketing and merchandising on the West Coast. We created a system that would help our national advertisers primarily, although we helped the Western ones, too. But the Western advertiser had his home office here and he had a lot more field representation, because the Western market was his home market, and from there he had branched out—as, for example, Del Monte had, or as Dole Pineapple had from Hawaii.

Fuller Paint, a San Francisco company, was a good example. Sherwin-Williams didn't have anywhere near the advantage of a Fuller Paint Company with its own stores and all kinds of public awareness on the West Coast. Sherwin-Williams benefited enormously by using our *Sunset* marketing reps to help them with in-store displays and maybe introduce their Western sales manager to a chain of hardware stores—anything to get the benefits of the advertising. We frequently did this with companies that weren't even advertising in *Sunset*, in order to show them how effective *Sunset* could be if indeed they did choose to advertise.

As marketing rep, I went out on the road every other week, alternating with my boss, Al Reasoner, the Eastern advertising director, who was based in San Francisco. We alternated between going up to the Northwest and going down to Los Angeles, working with the regional sales managers and calling on retailers. One day Mr. Reasoner said to me, "Your dad called me up to the office the other day and told me, 'I want you to make it as tough

A photo that appeared in the November 1953 issue of *Stet*, on the occasion of the 25th anniversary of Larry Lane's purchase of *Sunset* magazine, on October 12, 1928 (referred to here as Larry Lane's "birthday").

With his mother, wife, and son, Bill, Larry Lane displays the huge cake given him on his twenty-fifth anniversary as publisher of SUNSET. All the employees gathered on the patio to honor his "birthday" on October 12. Pictured on the cake was the cover of his first issue. Mr. Lane wears the badge presented to him by Howard Willoughby designating him "President, Publisher, Chairman of the Board, and Recreation Director".

on Bill as possible.'" My father was essentially saying, "Don't let Bill get away with anything." I don't think I would have tried, because I was working my tail off and I wanted to be the best at what I was doing.

I liked selling. In fact, I've always liked selling. Selling the magazine as a boy, I knocked on a lot of doors. As a youth, I sold white rats and I sold apples. My grandmother, when she lived with us at Quail Hollow in the middle 1930s, polished apples, and I sold them in Santa Cruz to grocery stores. We had a Red Bank apple, as we called it, a maverick apple that grew at Quail Hollow. I'd just gotten my driver's license, and I took them down to Santa Cruz in an old Dodge truck.

I like to win. I wanted the money, I suppose, but I just enjoyed it. I also like meeting people. Will Rogers had a famous line: "I never met a man I didn't like." Well, I really never have met a person I immediately *dis*liked. I just like people, and I like the satisfaction of doing something well that I have a knack for. And my dad, who was an outstanding salesman, was a great role model. I remember he helped me with my first advertising presentation, which was for Chambers gas stoves. We worked on it together quite a bit, trying to get the sequence of points exactly right.

In 1950, I went back to New York and opened our first *Sunset* office there. Mel went into production, and they sent him to a printing plant, R. R. Donnelly, in Chicago, and then later to Pacific Press in Los Angeles. I went back to New York with my father and Mr. Willoughby. We traveled by train and had meetings all the way across the country, with lots of discussions about the type of person we would like to hire to run the New York office. We ended up hiring Clifford Ensinger, who was Midwest manager for the *New Yorker*. It was a wonderful choice. He was a very fine professional, and I learned a lot from him. I was his first salesman, and then I helped hire a second salesman and a third salesman. For a small magazine on the West Coast, having three full-time people in New York was a big commitment. Subsequently we opened our own offices in other cities, beginning with Detroit, Boston, Atlanta, and Chicago.

I think back to 1950 and the scared young man from out West who came to New York to be *Sunset*'s first advertising salesman in that city and who did not have one gray flannel suit to his name. I lived in an apartment in midtown Manhattan, at Forty-eighth and Lexington, near Grand Central Station. This was Madison Avenue, the Big Leagues. At the time Dad sent me to New York, he had not been able to get Kodak, Pan American, or Best Foods for *Sunset*, and he said, "Bill, I want you to make those accounts your targets." And I got them all during the year and a half I was back there.

I'd be the first to say that timing is critical in any situation, whether it's marriage or any other kind of relationship. Coming along at the time I did, in 1950, a few years after the war's end and in the midst of a population explosion out West and the growth of the Western market, I was fortunate. But I would like to think that some of the things I did were effective. Each one of these accounts posed a different sales challenge.

Kodak had been in *Sunset* many years before. My father thought that I should tackle that one because of my interest in cameras, and also because of the sales challenge. On the Kodak account I did a number of things. I'm a prop man. I would rather not just rely on words, but have examples to prove a point. I came home at Christmas and took photographs down at my parents' ranch at Quail Hollow, where the grass was green in December and my mother had roses espaliered in front of the house. It was kind of chilly in the Santa Cruz Mountains, although it was a bright, sunny day. We had a large irrigation tank on the property where we swam in the summer when it was warmer—certainly not in the winter. But I persuaded Mel to get into the pool, freezing his you-know-what off, and I photographed him standing waist-deep. I made sure to get far enough back so that you couldn't see any goose pimples.

It was the early advent of Kodacolor, so I used some Kodacolor film. In the pictures I had Dad wearing an aloha shirt and holding a horse, and my mother was wearing a kind of lei. I went back with an assortment of these photographs of warm, sunny California in the winter, and fortunately when I got up to Rochester in January there was a hell of a blizzard going on. This fellow, the chief of Kodak advertising, said, "Well, Bill, how did your vacation go?" I said, "Fine. Here are some pictures I thought you might enjoy." He looked at them, amazed. In those days, most New Yorkers were used to thinking about warm, sunny Florida in the winter, but they were not used to thinking about California that way.

Kodak had a big developing studio over in the Stanford Industrial Park, and I took pictures of this big roll of Kodacolor prints coming off the machine. I also came armed with sales records that established that Westerners took a lot more photographs in the winter than the average for the U.S., even more than in the South. Maybe they have less wintry weather in the South, but in some parts there wasn't anywhere near the activity in photography you saw in the West.

One of the main challenges when dealing with any national advertiser in those days was to establish that the West was different. The pitch was, you were not going to have the same impact out West by using national media alone, even if you might have distribution there—and most magazines did have good distribution in the West. We stressed the point that Western readers were prime customers for many products, and that they were apt to look to *Sunset* first.

Pan American is a good example. We could show all kinds of passport figures and departure and arrival figures to make the case that Westerners, more than other Americans, were on the move. And, we reasoned, there was no better way to reach the Western customer than through *Sunset*. We used the fact that *Sunset*'s travel section had many travel agents who were actually advertising in *Sunset*, with their own money, and that the American Society of Travel Agents members here in the West were some of our best friends.

My year and a half in New York City was not only a solid success, but a great learning experience. *Sunset*, meanwhile, was taking off. Those years right after the war were very heady years, and the magazine was gaining acceptance. Like no other region of the nation, the West had been economically and demographically transformed by the war. People were building homes, and there was a tremendous migration to the West. *Sunset* benefited from the increased mobility, home ownership, and automobile ownership. In 1947 circulation passed 300,000; a year later it increased to 400,000. While I was in New York, it passed the half-million mark.

The postwar boom led to the rise of suburban communities, and the construction of ranch houses for upwardly mobile middle-class Westerners, the core *Sunset* audience. As *Sunset* reported heavily on this trend and identified with it, we began to consider a more suitable headquarters building and location for the magazine, one appropriate to its image, content, and readership.

Sunset, April 1953.

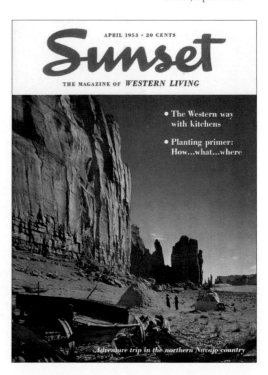

Even before I left for New York, the planning was under way. We looked at the Alta Mira in Sausalito, when that hotel came up for sale. We even considered the old Pullman house in Hillsborough, the Carolands Chateau. We finally decided to design and build our own structure on the peninsula about forty miles south of San Francisco. We found a magnificent seven-acre, oak-studded piece of land along San Francisquito Creek in Menlo Park, acreage carved from the old four-hundred-acre Timothy Hopkins estate.

The new headquarters was a long, low building designed by Cliff May along the lines of an early Spanish-California ranch house. It had a huge lawn and ample land for gardening areas, as well as state-of-the-art test kitchens inside. We moved into the new building in April 1951. *Sunset*'s new headquarters, known as the "laboratory of Western living," would become inseparable from the company's very identity. The move was reported as a news event by both *Time* and *BusinessWeek*, where it was presented as evidence of *Sunset*'s boldness and confidence. All the elements were now in place for the full flowering of Lane *Sunset*.

The West vs. the Rest

In 1952 my father went into semi-retirement, and the operating management of the Lane Publishing Company was turned over to Mel and me. In March of that year our names appeared on the *Sunset* masthead for the first time: Mel was business manager and I was advertising manager.

The announcement of my becoming advertising manager was an oddball thing that can only happen in a family business. I was advertising manager on the masthead (in September 1954 my title was changed to sales manager), but in fact I was in charge of editorial, advertising, and books, while Mel, as business manager, was in charge of production, manufacturing, and purchasing. In a family business we kind of jockeyed titles around, simply in order to let people know where the authority was.

Laurence Lane, flanked by Bill (left) and Mel, in a courtyard at *Sunset* headquarters in 1954.

I was in charge of the creative departments. When I came back from New York, I was an assistant makeup editor, working on the layout of the magazine. So I was beneath most of the editors, but it was pretty well understood that I was probably going to be managing them someday. In *Sunset* the Lanes were the true editors. A publisher in most magazines is a kind of super advertising director, but publisher of Lane *Sunset*—first my dad and then myself, and Mel in my absence—meant very definitely strong editorial oversight, whether it was books or the magazine.

I made editorial my number one priority. My father was not as interested in writing and practicing the trade of editorial as I was, with my communications background. I loved writing, and I got more involved in the nitty-gritty of editorial, the goose that lays the golden egg.

When Dad retired early, he felt very confident that I wouldn't make dramatic changes without going to him. For a number of years I reviewed every issue for the editorial department, and would run these critiques by my father. I remember going down to Quail Hollow one weekend when Dad was upset about some decision I had made, and I stuck to my guns. There were two or three such occasions. And there were lots of times in the course of our discussions when we couldn't agree on something and I had to hold firm. My attitude was, if I'm going to have responsibility, then I'm going to make the decision.

One decision that fell to me involved the fate of *Sunset*'s editor, Walter Doty. Walter was an advertising man out of Foote, Cone & Belding who had joined the magazine in 1939. My father wanted a new look for the magazine, and that was the reason he brought Walter in. The owner of the business at the time, James Webb Young, supported this choice. Walter was a very fine horticulturist, and gardening was *Sunset*'s most important editorial department in terms of holding the reader month in and month out with a dependency on the information that appeared in the magazine. You could go in and out of food, go in and out of homes, go in and out of travel, but gardening was steady. Walter, who was also strong on home design and food, came in with an avid interest in gardening, which he pursued at his home in Marin County and, later, after the company moved to Menlo Park, in Los Altos, and he brought this interest and expertise to the magazine.

When I came back from New York, one of my jobs was to phase Walter out. He was a wonderful editor, but it had gotten to the point where we were debating too many issues with him. In 1950, we had brought in Proctor Mellquist from *BusinessWeek* as managing editor, and we slowly turned over the management of the editorial department to Mellquist. Proc, as we called him, was originally from the Northwest, had worked as an advertising copywriter in New York, then as a magazine editor on *Look*, *Science Illustrated*, and then *BusinessWeek*. At some point my father said to me, "You know, we've got to make a change with Doty," and by then I was convinced that Mellquist was well qualified to become editor.

It was up to me to figure out what to do with Walter, who was carrying the title of editor but really did not have the final authority. Mellquist was managing editor and calling the shots, but to the outside world Walter, with his prestige and credibility, was still recognized as the top man. Rather than fire Walter or retire him early, as my father was inclined to do, I convinced Dad that there was a real opportunity for *Sunset* to take advantage of Walter's talents, and hopefully keep him motivated and very productive, by appointing him director of editorial research. It was certainly a good title to show on the masthead. Walter agreed to stay on in this new role, beginning in February 1954, and he proved to be very good at it.

More than any other magazine, *Sunset* did research on its audience in order to understand its readers, to make its readers more knowledgeable about what *Sunset* was about, and to make our advertisers more knowledgeable of what our readers were about, what they liked and what they didn't like. This was the *modus operandi* of Meredith Publishing, in Des Moines, and we carried on the tradition at *Sunset*, taking it far beyond even Meredith. I got into it even heavier than my father did.

A *Sunset* sales conference in New York City in 1958. Bill Lane stands in the center of the back row, with Proctor Mellquist to his right.

We conducted not only mail research but on-site home research. That's one of the ways I used Walter Doty as director of editorial research. In the city of Arcadia, for instance, in Southern California, we took every *Sunset* reader and then interviewed the resident next door, with similar income, similar lifestyle. We went into the town and just analyzed it upside down and backwards, did some mail interviews, followed up with personal interviews, talking to the husband and the wife.

Sunset readers, we found, were far more adventuresome, far more willing to take risks, far more interested in learning more. *Sunset* readers entertained more. There was more joint decision making, involving husband and wife, with regard to travel, decorating, gardening, and so forth. There was just a very dramatic difference. Westerners generally were more experimental, more willing to take chances. A lot of that had to do with the lifestyle of the West and also with the early settlement of the West. *Sunset* readers, our research showed, were the most "Western" of the Westerners. When you asked residents whether, given the opportunity, they would take the trip down the Colorado River, or accept the six free skydiving lessons, or whatever it was, the difference between *Sunset* readers and non-*Sunset* readers was just black and white. *Sunset* readers were much more rugged.

Sunset readers were also more innovative when it came to things like building a deck on a hillside or trying out a new recipe or a new flower, a whole host of things. *Sunset* readers played far less bridge. They played far less golf. They were far more open to creative ideas for, say, redecorating a room or closing in a carport to create a family room. Things that would just be a dud nationally, the *Sunset* reader would use it, would try it. The per capita investment in a *Sunset* reader's home was much higher.

Our research also showed that *Sunset* readers were the opinion leaders and the people of influence in their communities. And the higher up you went—in education, income, and occupation—the more pronounced *Sunset*'s leadership became. *Sunset* superiority in circulation and coverage mounted relative to the increasing level of influence in the community—in Rotary clubs, chambers of commerce, school boards, and so on. We had mountains of evidence to demonstrate that.

So we had tremendous interchange with readers, more than any other magazine, and it continued throughout my tenure at *Sunset*. In my last year as publisher, 1989–90, I bet I visited over a hundred homes and talked with the homeowners. We sent an eight-page survey out to about ten thousand readers, asking what they liked about *Sunset*, what they didn't like, how they compared it with other magazines. We had a constant stream of correspondence back and forth with readers, plus constant phone calling.

All of this reader research, of course, we used with advertisers. Gardening is a prime example. Gardening had very little advertising support. *American Home* gave gardening up, and *House and Garden* later folded, because there was very little advertising support. So to justify the amount of gardening coverage in *Sunset*, the number of times we featured it on covers, we had to establish with advertisers that our readers were very interested in gardening. And we did that, over and over again.

Another advantage *Sunset* had with advertisers was its outstanding circulation record. In the 1950s, *Sunset* obtained most of its new subscribers by using the charge account lists of leading Western department stores. We were tough on subscriptions—no credit, cash in advance, cash in renewals. We wanted that subscriber to be very, very committed to reading *Sunset*. That was the theory on subscriptions. We wanted that repeat readership and a demonstrated commitment. We could make the case to advertisers that because we had this committed, dedicated readership, they would always have continuity for their ad campaigns.

Sunset's circulation climbed past 700,000 in 1957. Advertising revenue grew from $587,486 in 1945 to over $5,000,000 in 1957, and kept mounting. As it did, the magazine grew in size. The year 1956 saw 336-page issues back to back in April and May, topped by a 340-page issue in 1960. Meanwhile, *Sunset* expanded geographically as well. In June 1952, seven years before it achieved statehood, Hawaii became part of *Sunset* territory, as *Sunset* took over the circulation of *Hawaii Farm and Home*, a magazine published by the *Honolulu Star-Bulletin*.

Sunset magazine's connection to Hawaii actually went back to its founding by the Southern Pacific Railroad, which had its own Southern Pacific Steamship Lines to increase commerce into the Pacific. Mel and I formed our own connection with Hawaii during World War II, when we were anchored together twice in Pearl Harbor, where we shared good family friends. We both liked Hawaii and considered it an exotic but logical extension of *Sunset* territory, but my dad needed convincing. Mel and I persuaded our parents to visit Hawaii before making up their minds. They did and they quickly came around to endorsing the idea.

Mel and I were part of a group of individuals who gathered in Hawaii in the early 1950s to promote travel and tourism in the Pacific Rim region, including Australia. The result was PATA (the Pacific Area Travel Association, later the Pacific Asia Travel Association) and PBEC (Pacific Basin Economic Council). *Sunset* was a founding member of both organizations, and I later served as president of PATA. In this and in other ways, *Sunset* contributed to a boom in tourism in Hawaii. Both the magazine and *Sunset* Books were pioneers in introducing Americans to travel opportunities in the Pacific, including exotic locales off the beaten path of most tourists. At the same time, in the 1950s, *Sunset*'s coverage of Japanese gardening, design, and cuisine opened up that country to Western readers.

Sunset also promoted awareness of Alaska. Here again it was a combination of *Sunset* tradition and Lane intuition. Alaska has ties to *Sunset*'s very first issue, which contained a major article on the Klondike. Postwar *Sunset* expanded its coverage of Alaska as a tourist attraction, publishing the first major travel book on Alaska. In later years, I worked with Governor Walter Hickel to help bring Alaska into the "travel family," you might say.

I happened to be in Alaska when President Eisenhower signed the act granting the territory statehood, on

TO HONOLULU FOR LUNCH? Bill Lane and a group of Bay Area executives hopped over and back in one day on Pan Am's special Intercontinental Jet Clipper Flight Sept. 1. They left S.F. Airport at 8:30 a.m., arrived back at 10:30 p.m. after a swim at Waikiki and lunch at the Royal Hawaiian Hotel with Hawaiian government and business leaders. Nancy Bannick, Hawaii Editor, took the photo as they arrived. Next to Bill Lane is William J. Mullahey, Pan Am Regional Director in Hawaii. Right is Herbert F. Milley, Pan Am Traffic Division Sales Manager.

A photo from the October 1959 issue of *Stet* shows Bill Lane arriving in Hawaii aboard Pan Am's Intercontinental Jet Clipper.

July 6, 1958. My wife, Jean, and I were part of a small group of about a dozen Americans traveling with West Tours, an outfit that converted old WWII Canadian gunboats into small tourist boats. Our group arrived in Ketchikan on the morning of July 7, and the place was dead. This was not the scene of jubilation I expected, so I asked our captain why Alaskans weren't celebrating their statehood. The captain explained that the locals had done their celebrating on July 6. Everyone was now sleeping it off.

As *Sunset* expanded, it remained true to the core mission described in its subtitle: *The Magazine of Western Living*. With a new editor in Proctor Melquist, a larger staff, and a bigger magazine, the editorial department became more ambitious. The magazine now routinely featured what some of us called the Big Essay, an in-depth, fact-filled treatment of a single subject, usually heavily illustrated with photographs and charts. Cover stories included the automobile and the eucalyptus.

There was predictability to the editorial content that readers could expect from each issue: informative articles and familiar columns about what

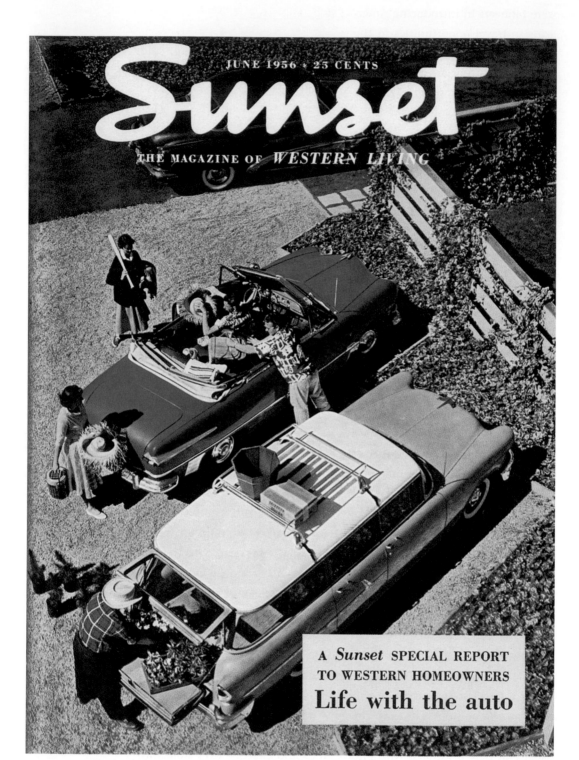

JUNE 1956 • 25 CENTS

Sunset

THE MAGAZINE OF *WESTERN LIVING*

A *Sunset* SPECIAL REPORT
TO WESTERN HOMEOWNERS
Life with the auto

Sunset, June 1956

I like to call "the four wheels of the car": gardening, travel, home, and cooking. Readability was paramount, with the table of contents always beginning on the first editorial page. Departments were always in the same relative place, and articles were always continuous, with no jumping the text to the back of the magazine.

"The Kitchen Cabinet," a collection of family recipes sent in by readers, continued to thrive. In the mid-1950s, readers sent in about 150 to 200 recipes every month; from these about one-third were selected for filing and eventual testing, while 50 to 70 recipes were tested in the *Sunset* kitchens each month. Also, the "Chefs of the West" column, begun in March 1940, became a favorite among male readers.

There was a policy book that was required reading for every editor. It was written by my father, and I rewrote it when I took over *Sunset*. That policy book was the bible for the editors. Among other things, it stipulated that every article had to guide the reader toward the accomplishment of an activity. "How to do it" meant how to complete the task. Each travel article, for example, was prepared with the assumption that the reader would make the trip and would desire a complete, step-by-step, how-to-do-it account of the conditions he or she would meet.

One often heard it said in those days, "When *Sunset* comes out, people take action." We made this our editorial concept from our very first issue of *Sunset*. Nothing is in it that can't be completed by readers. Maybe you can't eat papayas because they give you indigestion, or maybe you can't take a trip around the world because you can't afford it. But we knew from our own testing and research that a large number of our readers could do everything our editors wrote about in any issue: they took the trip, baked the cake, built the deck, and so on. *Sunset* was not passive, not just entertaining; it was enlightening and inspiring, and it was certainly instructive.

Long before it became a cliché to talk about business "solutions," *Sunset* was offering solutions to a lot of problems and challenges. We would hear from readers things like "My lawn's dying," or "My rosebush is dying," or "We had a fire in the garage and we need to remodel," or "I'm having a dinner party for eight," or "I'm thinking of building a deck." *Sunset* tried to be there with answers. One of our concerns was to help readers *anticipate* problems. One story we did on a great lake for fishing had as its lead sentence something like "The weather will be hot, the road will be terrible"—and then came the punch line—"but the fishing is great." The point was that you'd get good fishing, but you should anticipate bad roads, hot weather, dusty trails, mosquitoes, and so on.

In 1954, my father was quoted as saying, "A magazine should be a selective medium. It should pick out a specialty and stick to it." This was one of Dad's great pieces of wisdom. Hundreds of magazines bit the dust trying to be all things to all people. Selectivity both in editorial content and in readership continued to be the key to *Sunset*'s booming success in the 1950s and beyond.

Church and State

For those large issues of the magazine in the mid-1950s we were able to convince advertisers that *Sunset* was the equivalent of the *QE II*, so we had some very fine advertisers using relatively small space. In fact, we had to turn down advertising, because the presses at the time could handle only so many pages. *Sunset*'s content back then was about 60 percent advertising and 40 percent editorial.

Advertisers knew that through *Sunset* they could reach a select market, one with above-average purchasing power. We carried the tremendous volume of advertising we did at very high rates, with no frequency, no volume discounts, a much higher cost-per-thousand-readers. "As advertised in Sunset" was like a *Good Housekeeping* seal of approval—although we never developed a seal.

As the issues became much bigger, the pressures became much greater, since advertisers were becoming much more influential and advertising agencies began leaning on everyone. *House Beautiful* and *Architectural Digest* coordinated ads with advertisers. There's nothing wrong with that, but I was very much opposed to it. I practiced separation of church and state, in terms of not allowing advertisers to have an undue influence on the magazine. For one thing, we didn't have any position guarantees for advertisements. For years Southern Pacific wanted a left-hand page in the travel department, and we tried to do it for them, but we never guaranteed anything.

The most famous position guarantee in the history of the magazine industry was called the Campbell's Soup position. This was the first full page following the main editorial page, which in *Sunset* was the table of contents. We had never carried Campbell's Soup ads, but after the war, when *Sunset* became well enough established to attract national food advertisers, I remember paying a visit to Camden, New Jersey, where the advertising agency BBD&O had the account. BBD&O had many other accounts for *Sunset*, so we had a great deal of pressure on us to accept Campbell's Soup. But the only way we could get Campbell's Soup for *Sunset* was to guarantee that first full page following the main editorial page, always a prime advertising page—and I would not do it.

Advertisers have long tried to dominate programming and editorial content, and they have had to recognize—and certainly at *Sunset* we made it very clear to them—that they really were the beneficiaries of the main reason that people read a magazine, which is for the editorial content, not the advertising. The editorial gets people interested in a subject. They then turn to a source, a place they want to take a vacation, a product they want to buy to do the recipe, or the paint they want to use to paint the deck, or whatever it may be. We used to simplify it for advertisers by telling them, "Our job is how to do it, and yours is what to do it with."

Advertising space and editorial space had to be coordinated. Layout and mapping, as we called it, and it was a critically important job, and also a big job in the days before computers. *Sunset* makeup tried to coordinate the advertising with the very rigid departmentalizing of the editorial. For example, we tried to get garden advertising in the garden department. Travel came first in the magazine, followed by the general editorial section; then came home, food, and gardening. The sequence of these last three would change depending on the season. We always tried to match advertising and editorial as closely as possible.

But there was no commitment on editorial to the advertiser. We never let salesmen sell against editorial—meaning try to match particular ads to particular articles. We didn't want any collusion between advertising and editorial. In fact, if we had an article, say, on the South Pacific, and we had advertising for a cruise ship line on a South Pacific cruise, we would try *not* to position it with that editorial, in order to avoid any appearance of preferred positioning.

Most of our selling started with the premise that any section of the magazine was a good section. For one thing, we didn't start articles up front and then jump them to the back of the book. The garden department was probably one of the most popular, and that was in the last section of the magazine. We had a lot of research—a *lot* of research—that showed the flow of readers going, maybe, first to food or first to gardening, and it would vary according to the season. When they were planning vacations in the early spring, readers might go to the travel section first. The point is, eventually they got through the entire magazine, so position was not a crucial factor.

We always made a very concerted effort to get advertising content that would have credibility and relevancy to the reader's lifestyle. We strove to have advertising that really matched up, some of it by exclusion. *Sunset* barred beer and tobacco advertising starting in 1940, which complemented its long-standing ban on hard liquor ads. There was a list of items we would not accept, including feminine hygiene products because we were mindful of our male readership.

Many of the surveys we did proved that people enjoyed the advertising as much as the editorial content, because the advertising was typically geared toward helping readers act upon the ideas presented on the editorial side. In fact, a lot of the magazine's service was in advertising. In the surveys that we did, when we asked readers, "Which do you like the best, advertising or editorial?" *Sunset* readers always came out highest as liking both. Our readers did not resent advertising, because we made sure it was relevant and appropriate.

At the same time, we tried to keep the editorial pages as free as possible from brand identification. For many years we carried far more appliance advertising per issue than any other magazine. In our articles, we would do everything we could to mask the brand name of the product. For example, in a photograph showing food being cooked in a frying pan, we would pull in very close on the pan so that the photograph didn't show the burner, which may have been recognizable as one made only by Westinghouse or General Electric or Amana or whoever it was.

Sunset had some of its greatest growth during the decade of the 1950s because we impressed upon the national advertisers that their TV ratings were much lower in the West than the audience size they could reach with one ad in *Sunset*. This, too, we documented with all kinds of reader surveys. This was a time when television seemed to pose a threat to print, and national magazines like *Life*, *Saturday Evening Post*, *Collier's*, and *Look* were knocking their brains out trying to compete with television.

My dad was frightened by television, but I was fascinated by it from the beginning. With my severance pay from the navy not long after the war, I bought one of the first television sets in San Francisco, a Hallicrafters with a four-by-six-inch black-and-white screen—not too different from the radar screen I had been glued to for several years as a naval gunnery officer on a troop transport. The cost was $209. Hallicrafters was among the first to produce televisions, because they could turn what they were doing for ships right around into a civilian product. I made the purchase because I wanted to follow television and track its influence on the magazine industry.

I've always been excited about new technology. With the $30 I earned in my first summer job as a packer in the High Sierras, I bought a Gilfillan radio, very advanced with tubes and a speaker. Early in my *Sunset* career after the war, I produced the first audiovisual presentation with 35 mm photographs that I took, along with my own narration on a separate tape. Later, under my direction, *Sunset* pioneered the use of audiovisual presentations in the magazine industry. Later still, I started our Sunset Films division, which produced television films and videos for Chevrolet, Bechtel,

Royal Viking Lines, the State of Alaska, and other top clients. I was the first customer at my camera store to buy a Polaroid Instant Camera. And none of my friends would believe me when I sported the first solar-powered wristwatch they had seen.

My point is, I never felt threatened by television when it was on the rise in the 1950s. I got A. C. Nielsen to give me television ratings, and these revealed that viewership was much lower in the West. Per capita ownership of television sets was *higher* in the West, but this was deceptive as a measure of viewership because per capita income was higher. And with the California Ranch home spread out the way it was, there were multiple television sets per household. It made sense to me that television viewing went up in the winter in the Midwest, for example. Coming from the Midwest, I knew what winter was like, and this was long before the Midwest adopted cross-country skiing and snowmobiles and so on. It also just seemed inevitable to me that viewing would be off in the West, that Westerners would be watching less television in winter.

We got Nielsen's *regional* figures, which were not routinely released at the time, and sure enough, they showed that the ratings for all the popular shows were way down in the West. When television personality Arthur Godfrey read about some of the research I had acquired, he called on us at *Sunset*—arriving by helicopter on our lawn—because his ratings were down in the West, and he was trying to figure out why that was true.

In dealing with the competition from television, we were really selling the use of magazines regionally, not just *Sunset*. My dad was scared to death of Western editions of national magazines, particularly when *Better Homes and Gardens*, where he had started, created a Western edition. My exposure

Photos printed in the September 1956 issue of *Stet* show the celebrations at Sunset on the occasion of the fifth anniversary of the company's move to its Menlo Park headquarters.

3 staff members with the longest service records received gifts from L.W. Lane at 5th Anniversary celebration of SUNSET's move to Menlo Park. Left: Ebba Pehrson (39 years) receives a pearl necklace, Agnes Larson (30 years) a watch, Myrtle Pehrson (39 years) a pearl ring. Right: the Lane family ready to cut the Anniversary cake.

in New York helped to make me very much aware that as print was competing with television, we all stood to gain by banding together to sell the values of print.

I was always a great believer in the idea that the success of other magazines' regional editions would only help *Sunset*: that if those magazines were selling the Western market, then that was helping us with our job. After a while, we were spending less time establishing that the West was different and more time emphasizing why *Sunset* was superior to other types of media, including magazines focused regionally in the West. We just had to prove that we were doing a better job: *Sunset* would stay around the home longer, we would reach a greater combined male/female audience, we would be read more in schools, and we would be referred to more often as the authority in those fields that we wanted to be an authority in. These were the arguments we made, and we had the track record to back them up.

I am reminded how fast the hit parade can change, as I think back to the popular names everyone knew well during the years when our family was moving from Des Moines, Iowa, and settling in California. Our covered wagon going West in December of 1928 was a beautiful new Packard. Our first new car in California was a Franklin. We bought an Atwater-Kent radio and then a Gilfillan. We listened to *The Amos 'n Andy Show* and *Major Bowes' Original Amateur Hour*, and the Don Lee Pacific radio network, while glancing at Mutt and Jeff in the *San Francisco Call Bulletin*, with advertisements created, perhaps, by the Lord & Thomas Advertising agency. We ate our "Pearls of Wheat" cereal with cream-topped pasteurized milk, kept fresh in my mother's Bohn refrigerator. Every one of these brand names—and I could keep adding to the list—is long gone, yet the industries to which they belonged are stronger than ever.

My father used to say that it was harder to keep a good business going and profitable than to start one. Dad took over *Sunset* in 1928 and saw it through nearly a decade of Depression and then the war. By war's end, *Sunset*'s staff-written, how-to-do-it, home-owning, family-oriented content was in great demand, and the magazine was in a position to take advantage of the tremendous postwar surge of growth in the West.

The challenges facing second-generation management are different from the ones that the first generation contends with. I was very aware that loyalty would soon fade during a management transition if there was significant lack of confidence in the new team—and the sons of the boss are always especially suspect. Advertisers are very fickle with their tangible loyalty as magazine managements change. So are readers. The fact that we did not lose this confidence during the booming 1950s was a source of great relief and great satisfaction.

Over the course of the decade, my father was gradually stepping out of active management. At the end of 1959, he decided to hand the reins over to Mel and me, and he became chairman of the board. The masthead of the January 1960 issue of *Sunset* magazine designated Laurence W. Lane, Jr., as publisher of the magazine and Melvin B. Lane as publisher of *Sunset* Books.

Bill Lane at *Sunset* headquarters in 1972.

Chapter 3

Sunset Unlimited

Hearth and Headquarters

I was pretty happy as a bachelor during my *Sunset* apprenticeship. I belonged to the Bachelors Club and I socialized a fair amount, but Mel and I were just working our tails off. I had little time to date, let alone fall in love with a woman. But all that changed in the lobby of *Sunset* headquarters in Menlo Park on Saturday morning, July 24, 1954.

Dad, Mel, and I were getting ready to head to the Bohemian Grove, a private campground retreat north of San Francisco. A gal from Chicago named Jean Gimbel walked through the front door with her sorority sister from Burlingame. Jean was out west on vacation and wanted to see the new headquarters of the magazine. She had met a young lady I went out with a couple of times named Peggy Montgomery, in Southern California, and it was Peggy who suggested to Jean that she look me up.

Jean was a color stylist for the Martin-Senour Paint Company in Chicago. Martin-Senour was a Canadian company that advertised in *Sunset*. It, along with Sherwin-Williams, was in the forefront of all the paint companies in individual personalized color styling through a system that Martin-Senour patented. Jean was a graduate of Northwestern, where she took lots of art courses and majored in architectural drawing and rendering. She put her talents and training to good use at Martin-Senour, giving radio and television lectures to women's clubs in the Midwest about how to match paint with fabrics and about other matters of interior decoration.

My first meeting with Jean in the *Sunset* lobby was brief, but I knew I liked her very much. After she got back to Chicago, I called her up, first at the office and then at her apartment. She later said she thought I wanted more advertising from Martin-Senour and that I was using her as the vehicle to bring that about—but it wasn't long before she realized, "Something's up."

Our first date was in Chicago in September, in the presence of Richard M. Nixon, then the U.S. vice president. Nixon was the keynote speaker at an

Audit Bureau of Circulation conference. I decided I ought to attend the conference and I arranged to deliver a talk of my own. I phoned Jean and told her I was coming to Chicago and that I had tickets for the Nixon dinner, and asked her to join me. Afterwards we had drinks at the Palmer House.

After that first date we corresponded and telephoned, and soon enough Jean came west to look for a job. Our first date in California was a Stanford football game that autumn. We didn't even kiss when I said good night to her, but the courtship progressed rapidly, and by December we were engaged. We were married at St. John's Evangelical Church in Lincoln, Illinois, on April 16, 1955.

At first we lived in an apartment on Waverly Avenue in Menlo Park, not far from *Sunset*, and used bicycles to get around town. We moved a couple of times to other apartments nearby, but soon, with a family on the way, we were looking to build a home of our own. I asked Jean to scout out some property we might purchase in the foothill communities near Stanford. We wanted enough land for horse trails, as both of us were devoted horseback riders. Jean's search did not last long. She hiked up a hill in what would later be Portola Valley, saw the extraordinary view of rolling hills to the west and the San Francisco Bay to the east, and she knew she could stop looking.

We bought one piece of land, then acquired more land over the years until we owned almost ten acres, always with a sizable garden because Jean was an avid gardener. We built a ranch house on the property, on Westridge

Bill and Jean on their honeymoon in Hawaii in April 1955.

Bill and Jean Lane
and friend, in
Northern California
in the mid-1950s.

Drive, and moved in on January 17, 1957. That "we" included our first
child, Sharon, born the previous September.

Our home was designed by Cliff May, the Los Angeles architect who
had designed *Sunset*'s headquarters in Menlo Park. This blurring of the lines
between hearth and headquarters was a prime example of *Sunset*'s future
publisher practicing what he preached. We had located *Sunset*'s headquarters in a suburban setting, and had used residential architecture and landscaping to create a stimulating working environment that kept our staff
attuned to our editorial subjects and our readers' lifestyles. The new headquarters reflected not only the priority *Sunset* placed on home ownership,
but also its pioneering role in the fields of architecture and landscaping.

Cliff May had never done a commercial building before. But through
the urging of then-editor Walter Doty and garden editor Elsa Uppman
Knoll, and of course my parents, Cliff said he would take it on, and in
doing so he made architectural history. The new office was a long, low
building along the lines of an early Spanish-California ranch house.

In every aspect of our publishing home—site, architecture, building materials, furnishings, and plants—we conveyed our connection with the history of California and of Western America. The site was originally a portion
of the Rancho de las Pulgas, a Spanish land grant to Don José Arguello, governor of Spanish California in 1815. That era is reflected in Cliff May's architecture, which recalls California's early missions: a low, rambling style that
coordinates and engages indoor and outdoor areas. There were thick adobe

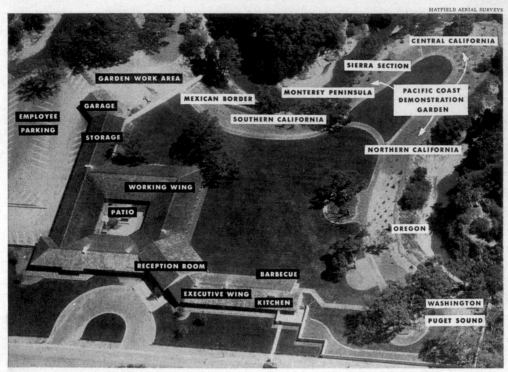

HATFIELD AERIAL SURVEYS

Aerial view of the Sunset *grounds in Menlo Park, looking south. Along San Francisquito Creek, which forms the irregular boundaries of the property to the west (right) and the south is*

Sunset's *demonstration garden. Here you can see, in a quarter mile garden walk, typical plants of Pacific Coast from Canada to Mexico growing side by side. Main entrance is at lower left*

On the next pages . . . we invite you on a walk through Sunset's new home

It's been a year this month since we moved to the country—to Menlo Park, 30 miles south of San Francisco. In our first year we've taken a lot of our own medicine in planning, gardening, and cooking in our new suburban home.

As we take you on a photographic tour, we're going to point out ideas which we feel could be adapted to many small Western homes. But this tour shouldn't take the place of a personal visit. Open house at *Sunset* is every work day—Mondays through Fridays, until four.

Like all Westerners who move to the country, we wanted elbow room. Our seven-acre site gives us new opportunity in garden experimentation and, incidentally, lets us do some office living outdoors.

A rambling ranch house structure fits our workaday needs. It also sits more easily than a conventional building under the

oak trees of our land on the bank of San Francisquito Creek, a piece of the old Spanish land grant Rancho de las Pulgas.

In working out our ideas in the *Sunset* building and its garden, we had the help of dozens of old friends—too many to mention. We'd like to thank them here for their encouragement and suggestions.

We were fortunate in finding sympathetic local craftsmen—woodworkers, weavers, metalsmiths—who made many of our fabrics, furniture, lamps, and other decorative pieces.

Cliff May, Los Angeles, designed the building. Associated with him were Higgins and Root, architects, San Jose. Our landscape architect was Thomas Church, San Francisco. Charlotte Hinckley, interior decorator, San Francisco, helped us with the furnishings.

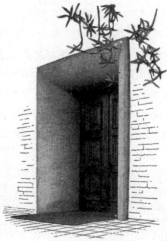

AUGUST 1952

47

The new *Sunset* headquarters, as featured in the August 1952 issue of the magazine.

Frank Lloyd Wright
exiting Sunset
headquarters with
Bill and Mel Lane,
on February 11,
1954.

walls, handmade desert tiles in the lobby and halls, a long, covered patio in
the tradition of the Spanish *corredor*, fifteenth- and sixteenth-century Italian and Spanish furniture, locally crafted lamps, benches, and tables, and
a collection of Navajo rugs—all brought together as part of a historically
unified setting.

It was Cliff May's achievement to blend a residential feel with the func-
tional needs of offices. Testimony to that achievement came in the form of a
warm endorsement by Frank Lloyd Wright. Wright had personally escorted
me through his famous home, Taliesin West, in Scottsdale, Arizona. I then
invited him to *Sunset* to talk to our editors. That evening, on February 11,
1954, in a speech he gave on the Stanford campus to a sold-out audience, he
raised eyebrows when he exclaimed, "*Sunset* magazine is the best building
I have seen all day!"

The idea of practicing what we preach extended to the grounds and the
gardens at the new headquarters, where the garden surrounds a 1.2-acre
lawn. The well-known landscape architect Thomas D. ("Tommy") Church
designed the gardens. Together with *Sunset*'s editors, Church laid out a garden that presented, in distinct areas, the major climate zones of the West.
The trees and shrubs represented *Sunset*'s territory, from Northwest rho-
dodendrons and azaleas to desert cacti and a tall yucca. Beds for annuals
and bulbs were replanted three or more times a year for constant displays
of color. All in all, more than three hundred kinds of shrubs, trees, vines,
ground covers, annuals, and perennials were growing in the garden at any

given time. Tommy Church also helped establish a test garden for use by the editors.

When we moved in, in 1951, *Sunset* staff members had offices and alcoves overlooking gardens, and editors had top-notch facilities, including a test kitchen and plenty of outdoor space to test and photograph garden, building, food, and craft projects. The new headquarters made news, which was no surprise; but what we were unprepared for was the onslaught of tourists eager to see it for themselves. We arranged guided tours, and *Sunset* became a regular stop for Gray Line sightseeing tours and a destination for field trips sponsored by garden clubs and many other groups. By the 1980s we received about 75,000 visitors per year.

In time, the headquarters expanded and evolved. In 1965, *Sunset* Books and the magazine's circulation department set up operations in a new 22,000-square-foot building, also designed by Cliff May, across Willow Road from the original building; the original building was now dubbed Willow South, and the new building became known as Willow North. The following year we added to Willow South a new four-station test kitchen, a large photographic studio, and a new photo library. In May 1973, as *Sunset* celebrated its seventy-fifth anniversary, we unveiled a spacious addition to the entertainment wing of Willow South: a new indoor-outdoor dining area, a large kitchen, a conference room, and a wine cellar. Later we would build a fitness center for our employees.

No wonder *Sunset* headquarters became known as a "laboratory of Western living." We tried to foster a work environment that was at once relaxed and highly productive. Long before the Microsoft "campus" in Seattle and, later, Google headquarters in Mountain View became celebrated for their employee-friendly work environment, *Sunset* had set the standard.

Breaking the Box

The design of *Sunset*'s headquarters reflected revolutionary developments in architecture, and *Sunset* was on its cutting edge. Beyond the influence of my parents, several people were responsible for this, starting with Walter Doty, who became *Sunset*'s editor in 1939; Walter's good friend Norm Gordon, *Sunset*'s brilliant art director from the late 1930s into the 1950s; and Elsa Uppman Knoll, our garden editor, who ran the Stanford garden school and was a favorite of my mother, who was herself a superb gardener.

Walter, during the years when he was Sunset's editor, was a great experimenter and had his own test gardens at home. Under his direction *Sunset* was the first publication to really get into landscape architecture and how it could be used in a residential way. Walter gave architects and landscape architects major exposure in the magazine. Tommy Church's work appeared in *Sunset* before Walter became editor, but under Walter's direction the landscape architects exerted a strong influence on home building. Walter not only had a horticultural bent, but he had a good sense of design and good taste. He made contact with and established good working relationships with leading architects, such as Mario Corbett, Pietro Belluschi, Harwell Hamilton Harris, and of course Cliff May, whose work *Sunset* definitely put on the map. Among the landscape architects, he worked with Tommy Church and brought Doug Baylis onto the magazine for a while.

The influence on home design was enormous. "Breaking the box" was an expression used to describe the dramatic reconfiguration of the home, more commonly known as "open planning." In those early days, if you put the living room in the back of the house instead of the front, where it was normally located, that was big news. The July 1940 issue of *Sunset* included a ten-page "Space for Living" section in which a group of younger designers, banded together in an organization called Telesis, looked at open planning and other aspects of houses and gardens of the future. *Sunset* did a series of articles on the ranch house. In 1946, this led to publication of the first large-format, hardcover *Sunset* book, *Western Ranch Houses*, written by Walter Doty and Cliff May and illustrated with houses May had designed. Our Cliff May ranch house book became the bible of that type of design, just as the ranch house itself came to symbolize Western architecture.

This was a time when *Sunset* was leading the way in so many aspects of home design: hot tubs, family rooms, island counter spaces, carports, skylights, larger eat-in kitchens, built-in appliances, glassed-in herb or kitchen gardens, and indoor barbecues, among other new ideas. In the late 1940s and early 1950s there were few readers, not even many professionals, and very definitely no national magazine editors who would have predicted the very enthusiastic response to all these elements only a few years later.

Sunset didn't invent new products or ideas, but we featured and encouraged them and thereby helped them to gain wide acceptance. We would come across a good idea and run with it before anyone else did. Sliding glass doors are a good example. Arcadia was the first manufacturer of sliding glass doors and the biggest supplier of them for years. An insurance man in Southern California saw it in a home right after the war. A homeowner had gotten a big piece of sheet glass—a commercial piece of glass at that time—built a wood frame around it and laid down some tracks. This door lent itself to the ranch home, of course, and Cliff May jumped on it.

Sunset featured sliding doors early and led with suggestions as to how they could be incorporated into a home. The attraction was that they erased the line between indoors and out, facilitating the concept of house and surroundings as a single integrated living space. And of course the opportunity to use sliding glass doors was greater in the West, where in winter that almost level surface from the indoors to the outdoors does not get obstructed by a bank of snow three feet high.

Another example was built-in appliances. Thermador, which was the pioneer in the field, was started by a homeowner who (against the building codes, I'm sure) took apart a regular freestanding oven and stovetop, put the stovetop in a tile surrounding (insulated, I hope), put the oven into a wall, and had a cabinet guy build some cabinets around it. The idea caught on, in part thanks to exposure in *Sunset*. And then General Electric and Westinghouse and Amana and other companies came along.

We were the first to promote what was then, in the 1960s, called the Radarange and is now called a microwave. *Sunset* had the first GE microwave, a huge thing that they trucked out for a demonstration for dealers. We published microwave recipes. General Electric gave out our microwave cookbook because people back then didn't know how to use the new appliance.

Sunset probably deserves special credit for promoting two related innovations. One was the open kitchen: the arrangement of the kitchen and dining room as one large space. *Sunset* editor Proctor Mellquist called the traditional separation of kitchen and dining room a form of "aping the manor house," evoking a time when cooking and serving were performed by servants: "a pretentious dining room, with a door to the kitchen and chairs around the table, and serving from left to right, with the housewife changing roles and being the maid and constantly getting up and then sitting down again." That "whole rigamarole," as Proc called it, was tossed out with the introduction of the open kitchen, which integrated the kitchen into the rest of the house—a concept featured in numerous articles in *Sunset*.

The other idea was incorporating the family room: creating a low counter separating the family room from the kitchen, so that the mother could work in the kitchen and see the children—and at that time a lot of our readers had young families. Today this arrangement is quite common, but it was rather revolutionary then, when kitchens were considered separate rooms, and family rooms were often thought of as libraries.

Another innovation we championed in home design was the so-called reverse plan. The traditional arrangement was to have a garden in front of the house along an entry path from the street with neat plants on each side, another element borrowed from the manor house and usually one that required a lot of maintenance. What happened under the influence of Tommy Church—and was then adopted by many people, including many architects—was to design the house with a reverse plan. The living area no longer faced the street, but instead was moved to the side or the back of the house. The landscape in the front of the house looked attractive but typically required little maintenance. This enabled the extension of the floor plan of the house by using the land as living area, with landscape architecture and house architecture working in tandem.

A lot of homes at this time were built in a U shape, and many had carports. Here again you could separate the West from the rest of the country, because that type of architecture, and the carport, were unique to the West, where the climate made it feasible. Another Western innovation pioneered by Tommy Church and first recognized in *Sunset* was the deck. We take it for granted now, but historian Kevin Starr rightly calls it "perhaps the Far West's most notable contribution to domestic architecture after the Spanish-inspired patio." Here was an essential and uniquely Western extension of outdoor living space, often onto hillsides and waterfronts.

Sunset is also credited with pioneering the later nationally popular A-frame design, championed out west in the 1950s by Henrik Bull. Here again, we didn't anticipate the A-frame, but we thought it made good sense when you looked at its accessibility for families who wanted to have a mountain home, particularly if they could get a Forest Service permit to erect a vacation home. It wasn't quite a do-it-yourself project, but for any handy person, with another helper, it was virtually a home you could build yourself. The large number of beach houses and mountain cabins in the

The three Lane couples (left to right): Bill and Jean, Larry and Ruth, and Mel and Joan, on the lawn at Sunset headquarters, circa 1956.

West are testimony to the fact that the West has been the nation's most active second-home market, in terms of both ownership and the opportunities in creative new design.

Quail Hollow, my parents' ranch in the Santa Cruz Mountains that they purchased in 1937, reflected many of these developments in home coverage in *Sunset*. By the 1950s, they had transformed their small family farm into a textbook version of the long, low Western ranch house, with gardens serving as outdoor living space. This was not something my parents did self-consciously; it was merely a reflection of their, and *Sunset*'s, taste. As historian Susan Lehman has written of Quail Hollow: "By the time the Lanes sold the ranch in 1954, the magazine's concept of informal, outdoor family living, houses built low, open and accessible to the outside, and landscaping with plants best suited for the geographical areas were an accepted way of life for millions of Western residents."

In 1958, these increasingly popular home design ideas, most of them postwar innovations, were incorporated into a revised version of Cliff May's *Sunset* book *Western Ranch Houses*, which became the definitive edition.

The Changing Western Home

One of the premier home award programs in the country is the American Institute of Architects–*Sunset* Magazine Western Home Awards, judged by a top professional jury and published biannually and exclusively in *Sunset* since 1956. We first did a trial program in 1956 with *House and Home*, a trade magazine then owned by Time Inc. They wanted to look at regional architecture and the region they wanted to begin with was the West. They were a little nervous about taking it on alone, so they asked us if *Sunset* would do it with them.

Perry Prentice was the editor of *House and Home*. Prentice was a very close friend of Cliff May's, whose homes he published in *House and Home*. Cliff convinced them that *Sunset* would be a good partner for them. There was a lot of pressure on some of the Time executives to go with a national magazine, such as *Better Homes and Gardens*, *American Home*, *House Beautiful*, or *House and Garden*. Aside from the national publicity that it would generate in *House and Home*, collaborating with *Sunset* would limit their visibility for that year pretty much to Western America. That was a decision which obviously worked to our benefit, and I always had a soft spot in my heart for Time Inc. as a whole and particularly for Perry Prentice, who sold that strategy to his management, who weren't quite as enthusiastic about it as he was.

In any event, we did it, and it was very successful, generating more reaction from that joint effort with *Sunset* than from any other previous collaboration. The architects were enthusiastic, and we had more readers writing in. It just caused a lot of commotion. And it happened at an exciting time in architecture. Bill Wurster, Henrik Bull, and all kinds of talented people were just coming onto the scene, and two or three great architects in the Northwest, two or three in Southern California.

I decided to institutionalize the awards program as a way of establishing leadership credibility for *Sunset*. So we approached the Western regional chapters of the AIA. We had a couple of meetings at *Sunset*, and then Proctor Mellquist and I traveled to Salt Lake, Portland, Tucson, and so on to attend the regional AIA membership meetings, and they all said they would like very much to do it on a regular basis. We had to get them whipped up because we wanted them to enter the best, most winnable homes in the *Sunset* competition instead of sending them to *Better Homes and Gardens* or *House Beautiful* or whatever.

Proc and I went back to Washington together and got the permission of the AIA executive board and a commitment that the board would endorse the approval of the Western regional chapters for this biannual awards program. We needed the board's sponsorship in order to be able to use the initials "AIA": "The AIA–*Sunset* Magazine Western Home Awards." The advantages to *Sunset* were enormous. It gave *Sunset*'s editors an early look at the latest innovations in home design. As testimony to the magazine's leadership position, many of the homes that first won awards in the *Sunset* program later received national awards. *Sunset* helped launch the careers of many talented architects by publishing their work for the first time. We probably published more new and experimental residential designs than other popular magazines. Of course, many homes that were entered in the AIA program did not get awards, but one of the rationales I had for taking the program on, beyond the credibility that *Sunset* gained from the competition, was that having those entries gave us a wonderful collection of homes for the magazine.

We also imposed some definite criteria, which some of the architects didn't like too much. For example, we made it clear that we would exert an influence on *how* we published their homes, and that would be based in part on what we felt was their livability. This meant that if they wanted to win an award, they couldn't do it just by putting forward unique architecture. They also had to take into consideration the livability of that home, how a family would be able to enjoy it. Frequently, for instance—especially in those days, but it's still true today—a lot of beautifully designed homes would have all kinds of glass. So then you run up against the family's concern for privacy.

To put it another way: the house might have admirable architectural features, but we were going to be very concerned with functionality—how

OCTOBER 1957 ★ 25 CENTS

Sunset

THE MAGAZINE OF *WESTERN LIVING*

American Institute of Architects · Sunset Magazine
WESTERN HOME AWARDS
28 Award-Winning Western Homes

Sunset, October 1957.

the kitchen worked, how the storage facilities worked, and so on. Sunset's emphasis was largely upon families, so we had to take into account the relationship of the master bedroom to the children's rooms, for example, and whether there was a family room—generally, how the family would actually use the home and whether they would find it to be a livable home. For an awards competition, the premium placed on livability was really quite revolutionary.

We also emphasized site orientation, and this was where Tommy Church had such an influence. He served on the first jury and then on four more after that. Each jury included a landscape architect. Other landscape architect jurors were Bob Royston, Pete Walker, Larry Halprin, and Ed Williams. The seven-member jury always included four architects, one landscape architect, one good professional from outside the field, and one layman, a *Sunset* editor. For the first eight programs Proc was that layman juror.

So site location was important, not only with respect to the view but also with respect to the wind and the afternoon sun. These and other considerations about how the home was sited were among the criteria included by the judges. Tommy Church, with his enormous prestige, forced the discussion of the siting of the building and forced the discussion of the development of the site. In other words, you couldn't ignore the house beyond its wall lines, which architects sometimes do. They're far more interested in structure and in interior space. Tommy Church, and the landscape architects after him, looked beyond the house as a structure. In Proctor Mellquist's words, "What *Sunset* advocated was that the house and the land be designed as a unit, in which the planning begins at both the view lines and the lot lines, not at the building line, and living areas can be outdoors as well as in."

We also began to give attention, in judging home design, to environmental issues. Our chief experimental area, beginning in the 1970s, was in energy conservation, particularly solar heating and cooling as part of the architecture of the house. This followed the oil shock of the early 1970s, so energy was very much on everybody's mind. In fact, this consideration would later influence the design of the third *Sunset* headquarters building, built in the late 1980s, also on Willow Drive, and known as Willow West. It incorporated passive solar heating and the imaginative use of natural light.

The AIA–*Sunset* Magazine Western Home Awards program was the first such competition to include remodeling and recreational homes as separate categories. We did a lot more on remodeling than other magazines, which focused more on new construction. "Remodeling" meant taking an existing home and improving it, either enlarging it to accommodate a growing family or modifying it in a way that made it a more livable home.

Carports are a good example. You could enclose the carport and make it into a family room, or create a master bedroom from the carport and then take the former master bedroom and make it a family room. There were all kinds of possibilities.

Architects had an immediate response to the AIA-*Sunset* awards, and manufacturers who advertised in *Sunset* did as well. In the building field it lifted the magazine to another level of acceptance and credibility, establishing *Sunset*'s reputation with a national audience. *House Beautiful*, *House and Garden*, *Better Homes and Gardens*, and *American Home* were all very popular, and they were much better known to the advertising community and the building and design field. But *Sunset* was now on the map.

One of our limitations, aside from being regional, was that we didn't go heavily into interior decorating, which *House Beautiful* and *House and Garden* did. We always made it clear that interior decorating was not our field, that we were not expert at it. Interior decorating would benefit indirectly from what we did, because you don't remodel your kitchen without buying new appliances. You buy paint and wallpaper and so on. So the advertiser has the opportunity to provide the what-to-do-it-with complement to the *Sunset* editorial content.

Proc Mellquist did some leadership articles on architecture, one of them called "The Changing Western Home," which ran in the May 1971 issue of *Sunset*. He and I worked together on it, but the inspiration for it and the thinking behind it were his, and it was a landmark article. Proc wasn't as chummy with some of the architects as Walter Doty was, but he understood the field.

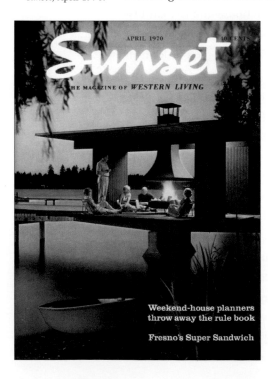

Sunset, April 1970.

One trend that came along in the 1970s was the idea of pavilions: homes made up of a series of separate units, or modules. This was the so-called engawa concept, and we parlayed it into showing the influence of the Orient. I got so enthusiastic about it that we built a model home up east of Sacramento, off Highway 50, called the Discovery House, a concept we had introduced in the early 1960s. We worked with two architects, and of course Proc. It was in a development called El Dorado Hills. It was a very exciting house, and before it was put up for sale we bussed advertising people up from the Bay Area, and we had a sales meeting up there, and did a lot of entertaining in the house.

The *Sunset* Discovery House was a real benchmark for us, although model homes were nothing new, not even for *Sunset*. Dad had a model home in the thirties over in Berkeley. *Sunset* and three hundred women, members of the Berkeley Women's City Club, got together to design a house. And subsequently *Sunset* asked them to do another house, in Park Hills, Berkeley, with architect Clarence Mayhew and landscape architect H. L. Vaughan. That house was featured in the March 1939 issue of *Sunset*.

Sunset rarely published the complete details on a home. We published kitchens, we published baths, we even published hallways, but it was really only in the AIA contest every other year that we would feature an entire house. Our books frequently had complete homes in them, but the strength of the magazine was its focus on particular *aspects* of a house, especially kitchens. That was another rationale I had for establishing the AIA relationship. Proc and I both felt that this would get us brownie points with the architectural fraternity, whose members were sometimes not too happy with us because we would come in and cherry-pick their homes. We'd pick a kitchen or we'd pick a deck or we'd pick this or that, whereas their desire was to have their entire home featured.

For each biannual AIA–*Sunset* Western Home Awards competition we would receive maybe three hundred or four hundred entries, and there would be about twenty awards. The other entries were in many cases homes that we were very interested in, even though the judges may not have found them to be award-worthy. A home could have a great kitchen, or it might have a great children's bunk facility, for instance.

There was also the matter of how the home was photographed for *Sunset* magazine. We would usually go out and re-shoot, but of course the architects would have preferred to use their own photographers to show off their home to the best advantage. I have in mind photographers such as Julius Shulman, a famous interior architectural photographer. In fact, generally speaking, *Sunset*'s artistic layout wasn't the most comfortable fit for the AIA people, at least not initially. But after we got it established and it became so popular with the architectural community, pretty soon we didn't have to urge the architects to save their best homes for us. They knew they would just get a bigger response from having a home published in *Sunset*.

Sunset's insistence on control was one reason we never established a close relationship with Joseph Eichler. In contrast to Cliff May's homes, which were, you might say, Spanish traditional, Eichler's were modern futuristic. For example, he used the inverted rooflines that gave you height at the perimeter rather than at the center of the home. And there were a lot of interesting concepts in Eichler's architecture, such as the atrium home. They offered quite a contrast to the conventional tract homes of the day, and they set a standard for an exciting new form of architecture that was noted nationally.

I knew Eichler very well. He started in Palo Alto, and in fact some of our editors lived in Eichler homes, and we were among the first to publish Eichler, helping him get national attention with his homes. But we were not as much into Eichlers as we were into the more traditional homes. There was also a clash of personalities. I liked Eichler myself, but he was a headstrong guy and he rubbed both Walter Doty and Proctor Mellquist the wrong way. He wanted to have things his way, didn't want his homes to be reported in any way but his own, as he was allowed to do in *House Beautiful* and one or two other magazines, but that was something we just didn't want to do.

Sunset didn't print as much color as architects or homeowners would have liked. They had beautiful carpeting and beautiful drapes and so on and so forth, yet we would show it in black and white. The reason in part was that we could just put a lot more information in black and white than if we printed it in color. Here I was influenced to some extent by my experience as a gunnery officer on my troop transport ship during the war. We did research on the quickest way to communicate—and remember, many kids on the gunnery crews weren't even out of high school. The quickest way you could teach those kids about how to assemble or disassemble or repair a gun was by using large type that was illustrated by line drawings. The next most effective way was using black-and-white photos. The least effective method was with four-color photos, because color gets in the way of the instructions.

So I never worshipped color. I think it has eye appeal, certainly on the cover and especially from a distance on the newsstand. But aside from the higher cost of color, if you're trying to instruct somebody on how to plant a tomato bush, you can do it a hell of a lot more effectively with line drawings or black-and-white photos than you can with a little postage-stamp-size color illustration. You can get a lot more information on the page. You can print smaller black-and-whites and more easily communicate the way a stairwell works, for example, than if you have to deal with color. I saw a lot of value in color for an opening article in the garden or food department. If you want to entice somebody to go to Hawaii, then there's a good argument for color. But I thought there was a place in a service magazine for black and white.

That's not to say that we shied away from new technology—just the opposite, in fact. *Sunset* was one of the first magazines in the entire country to put in an ATEX computer system for every senior editor, thus providing direct linkage for word processing composition of text and transmission to the printing plant. And when color came along, and litho-offset, we were at the head of the pack, working with Time Inc. in an experimental press in Los Angeles, Pacific Press, which Time owned and was testing. They were using it for covers on *Fortune*. I learned about it and got the director of production for *Time* to let us print, and then we got the printing plant to put in a press similar to it for litho, which allowed us to print four-color throughout the book. We started four-color printing in editorial in 1964.

Another *Sunset* difference was that our photographs had hardworking captions. As the magazine grew bigger, we had more space, and we began to use captions with a lot of substance and text to them. Not only did we give photographs the one-line caption, which might be all caps or italics or whatever, but we conveyed a good deal of information in the captions. Not just "This is a room in Joe Doakes's house" or "This is a remodeled

End shelves hold stereo receiver, cook books

Recessed ceiling lights

Original double-hung window

Speaker

China cupboard has glass doors on both sides

Backsplash is faced with mirrors

Strip lighting

Generous storage

island with cooktop

Dishwasher

New double-glazed windows and matching French doors open to terrace

Storage wall accommodates double ovens, microwave, and freezer-refrigerator

DON NORMARK

Bright *and spacious, new kitchen blends into family sitting room and dining area. It opens through French doors at right to terrace, pool*

An example of a hardworking photograph in *Sunset*, from the March 1982 issue.

living room." I always told our editors, Get your captions so they really tell a story.

We also did text *within* the photographs. You saw that predominantly when there was a listing of new American roses, or varieties of tomatoes, or whatever it might be. There would be text to go with that photograph, so that it was a *working* photograph—working in the sense that it conveyed not only the visual impression, but also textual information. We would put captions on top of a beautiful photograph because we knew from reader research that our readers liked it, that they got more out of an article on different types of garden shears, for example, because we made those photographs very hardworking, with captions both within and adjacent to the photographs. Gardening and food pieces benefited most from the use of these working captions, building articles only occasionally, travel articles rarely.

Sunset was always regarded as a little like a scissors-and-paste-pot operation by some art directors and magazine people in New York. But we understood our readers and how best to serve them.

The *Sunset* Family

The reader that we constantly strived to reach was the homeowner who had made the commitment, had the financial credibility to finance a home, had that home as a collateral asset, and was by every measure the best market for most of the products that we wanted to include in the advertising pages of the magazine. These were the people who most needed our help, and we were a service magazine. People who live in condos or apartments can't remodel even if they want to. There's no way they can knock out a wall, put in a patio, put in a skylight, and so on, if they live in a common dwelling. Ours was not a magazine for people looking to get more enjoyment out of their apartment.

A family home service magazine is by and large for families living in homes, but there was no prohibition that said we couldn't be read by somebody living in a condo, and in fact we were. If you went into the better multiple-housing developments, you would find a lot of *Sunset* readers. They bought more issues on the newsstands, particular issues with content that interested them. They were more selective, so they didn't want a continuous subscription. They purchased *Sunset* books. Many would own a barbecue book because they could barbecue on the patio of their condo or apartment. *Sunset* also attracted people who dreamed

The four Lanes at a ceremony to mark the tenth anniversary of *Sunset*'s move to its Menlo Park headquarters.

of owning a home. It's the same dynamic that's at work with people who buy *Western Horseman* yet don't own a horse but someday hope to, or others who buy *Pilot* magazine because they someday want to fly or they just like planes.

The essential ingredient for us was family. I've referred to the interviews we've done with readers over the years, and oftentimes we would get feedback about their attachment to *Sunset*, statements such as "I take *Sunset* to bed," or "I enjoy reading it in the bathroom," or "I took it on vacation," or "It's part of the family." "Part of the family" was always the most meaningful comment I would hear. You never heard it said that NBC was part of the family, or the *San Francisco Chronicle* was part of the family, but you did hear it said about *Reader's Digest* or *National Geographic* or your favorite magazine, whatever it might be. Magazines have that capability. If they do the best job they can, they will gain a franchise that will make that magazine a "part of the family." That is one of the unique features of a magazine, even today.

Every article in an issue of *Sunset* magazine, every page in a *Sunset* book, was published with a concern and respect for meaningful family experience. Editorial and advertising content was very carefully attuned to what we felt were the interests and tastes of the *families* who read our publications. In a very real way, not only were we relating to critical and specific problems in the environmental and social areas, but more importantly, we were also committed to helping the members of the Western family to share rewarding experiences, to gain greater values from life at home, and to better understand their own country and the world. That idea may sound romantic, but it was fundamental to our publishing mission.

There were never any promises that *Sunset* was going to save your marriage, or bring your family back together again, and yet we had countless examples of readers telling us how we brought their families *closer* together—for example, letters from a family who had a wonderful vacation together, inspired by an article in *Sunset*. One reader mentioned how an article on the Santa Monica Mountains had served to bring him and his son back together—he slipped it under his son's door and it got them talking about it.

Our sensitivity to the needs of family led us to push for convenience, though always in a way that allowed for quality and for some degree of personal input. Gardening is a good example. Tommy Church's gardening was low-maintenance gardening, aimed at people who were busy but wanted a nice garden. The same applied to *Sunset*'s coverage of cooking, which was presented as a unifying family "team effort." *Sunset* recommended that families cook together whenever possible, that teenagers be taught how to cook. We encouraged family vacation time, publishing recipes for campfire cooking or simple summer dishes to be enjoyed in mountain cabins or cottages by the sea. And we were always very big on family picnics.

Our definition of "family," in keeping with the times, came to include unmarried couples living together. Not that we were blatantly trying to identify with them, but we recognized that they were part of our audience. This was yet another way the West was different.

One of the things we promoted with advertisers was the useful long life of magazines, the large bonus readership that continues long after the magazine has appeared in print. In order to extend that life, we sold indexes. I started this early on when we began to publish the index. I went down to the Los Angeles Public Library and got permission to use their indexing system. We had to create separate indexes for our three, later four, regional editions, because each edition had different content. At that time only one or two other magazines published an index: *National Geographic* and, I think, *Scientific American*. We got very good feedback on the index from readers, and we sold thousands of bound copies.

We tried to discourage readers from ripping up the magazine to save articles. We wanted to keep the magazine whole, which is why we worked so hard on selling the annual indexes. We tried to preserve the whole magazine because, among other things, a reader at some point might want to refer back to an article he saw on, say, cruises in Alaska. Or a year from

The Lane family, with children Sharon, Brenda, and Bob, at *Sunset* in 1966.

The Lane family in December 1969, with children Sharon, age 13, and Bob and Brenda, ages 9 and 7.

now you may want to refer back to one of the fall issues on what you could plant at that time of year. What got torn out most frequently, we found in research, was recipes. People would cut them out and put them on a card, or they might put them in a folder designated for recipes for chocolate cakes or whatever it might be. People came up with ingenious ways of filing.

The family image of the magazine was reflected in our advertising. I've mentioned that we accepted no ads for hard liquor and that from 1940 on we stopped tobacco and beer. We had a list of some two dozen categories for which we would not take advertising. Advertisers carry this kind of cocky attitude that they are the power behind the throne of successful media, because they think that by withdrawing their advertising, or by threatening to do so, they can make you give in to their pressures. When we rejected advertising, it was always kind of a shock to the advertisers that we would do so.

I turned down the National Rifle Association, the NRA. That was back in the early 1980s, when the NRA was looking to soften its image. They came to us with a campaign that our staff had accepted because the executive vice president, Jack Henning, a wonderful guy who was a hunter, saw no problem with it. But he knew I might be sensitive to it, and anything that was questionable they brought to me. I said, "Not on your life will we accept that." It was a series of ads taking up multiple pages. Unfortunately, my decision brought me into conflict with two very close friends: one was Wally Schirra, the astronaut, with whom I had served on the National Park Board in Washington; the other was Victor G. Atiyeh, the governor of Oregon. I just didn't believe in what the NRA was doing in undermining the control of handguns. That was at the time when these sophisticated automatic repeating weapons were becoming available, and my wife was very much in the campaign to restrict handguns.

As it turned out, the advertising agency threatened to sue us, and I said, "Well, go ahead and sue us." We'd had that threat before. On several occasions I told people, "Fine, sue us; we'll get more publicity out of it even if we lose, and I don't think we'll lose." The NRA came back and said, "We'd like a survey of your readers." I said, "Fine." I went to my secretary and my wife, and two or three other people, and I sent back a letter that we had conducted this survey, and it was unanimous that our readers would object to ads by the NRA.

They came back and said, "Who are the people?" And I told them it was really just a survey of my immediate staff and family, but that there was no question in my mind that if I posed the question to our readers, they would object to it too—in *Sunset*. I said, "They might be hunters, or smokers, but they expect something from this magazine, and we are the publishers."

That was always the distinction I tried to make to my editors: that what we put in the magazine was what a person might do in public, versus what they might do in private. My father, for example, was an avid cigar smoker until well into his years out here, but he wouldn't publish tobacco ads in the magazine. We were creating an image there, and it had nothing to do with whether we ourselves drank or smoked or hunted. The image of the magazine had to reflect what you would expect of your minister, regardless of what his personal habits were. For example, presumably you trust your garage mechanic as a mechanic, to get the job done on your car. You really don't care whether he's sleeping around or not. You *would* be concerned if he showed up at work drunk or on drugs, but you're not too

concerned about his morals. It varies by the relationship that we have, and people had very strong expectations of *Sunset*.

The family concept extended to the entire *Sunset* staff. Employees used to speak of the "*Sunset* family," and we liked it that way. We had little turnover among the staff, which reinforced the sense of family. We had no names on the doors, no reserved parking lots. We didn't outsource any services, such as gardening or the mailroom. There was no *Sunset* type of person working at the magazine, but rather an enormous range of people, and we were willing to have management move people around the organization in order to find the right fit—another very family idea. When it occasionally happened that a Sunset staffer ran into financial difficulties or health problems, Mel and I did what any family member would do: we helped them out, discreetly of course. I remain convinced that the root of *Sunset*'s success was its thoroughgoing family nature.

At the core of that family were Mel and I. In 1960, when he and I took over the business, we created a holding company, Lane Publishing. It owned a cattle ranch in Northern California and some real estate on the peninsula. The book company was established and run by my brother, and I had the magazine company. We lived with that for a while, but we found that it broke down the two-way street of communications and it built up competition between our staffs. Different growth percentages were being compared. This was something we didn't like. We did not think such competitiveness was in the best interest of the company, so we put it all back together. We were a people business. We had to have an all-out team effort.

Mel and I spent quality time alone together away from *Sunset*, often at the Bohemian Grove, north of San Francisco, where we could discuss our family business. There were no agendas or note taking, only relaxed and bonding conversations to iron out wrinkles and ponder the future of our enterprise. We were adamant about not diverting money or talent from the two activities that were the backbone of our business: the magazine and the books. Very basic to our management was to set tough guidelines for expanding only by synergistic opportunities—staying in areas where we were authorities and maintaining our leadership in those areas. Mel and I took special pride, as did our mother, Ruth Bell Lane, when the Magazine Publishers Association selected *Sunset* as the recipient of its annual Henry Johnson Fisher Award in 1974, the first wholly family-owned magazine to be so honored.

A Three-Legged Stool

On February 20, 1967, a few days short of his seventy-seventh birthday, my father passed away after a brief illness. His spirit continued to live on in *Sunset*, even as the company expanded and thrived in ways he had not anticipated.

Mel Lane, Mrs. L. W. Lane, Mr. L. W. Lane, Bill Lane

The Lane family in a photo that appeared in the pages of *Stet*, the staff newsletter, in August 1963, on the occasion of the 35th anniversary of Lane ownership of *Sunset*.

VOLUME 15, NUMBER 12   LANE MAGAZINE & BOOK CO., MENLO PARK, CALIFORNIA   MARCH 3, 1967

February 20 Was Beloved Publisher Larry Lane's Last "Closing Date"

I have more than 30 years of memories of Larry Lane.

In my mind, hundreds of pictures of Larry and Ruth slide by to relive those years: on a hilltop in Los Altos; in the early days at Quail Hollow—breakfasts in the old kitchen, helping with the dishes, making cider; talks on the commute train; Montgomery Street, 5th floor, Montgomery Street, 6th floor; in a Navy hospital—pictures bright and pictures dark.

My thoughts now keep going back to the 1940's. In some ways, I think, these were the most exciting years in Larry's life. I know they were in mine.

These were the years when only Larry knew that SUNSET was on its way. SUNSET even then was something no one had seen before—a small magazine with more guts, integrity and pride than the biggest of the big magazines. And they were Larry's guts, integrity and pride.

Some advertisers recognized the strength of Lane's SUNSET, but in the eyes of too many advertisers it was just another little magazine, susceptible to the many kinds of advertising pressures.

I can still see him spoiling for a fight, to prove the bigness of this "nice little magazine." And during his fight to prove it, I grew to know him.

I remember the little things. An article on lighting fixtures concluded that about the only improvement made by the industry over the candle was to develop fixtures that gave us a headache more quickly. Following publication Larry was visited by representatives of the industry. There was no retreat or apology. "Our editors write as they please." I know that Larry felt we could have been just as helpful without the smart crack, but he did enjoy

March 5, 1890 — February 20, 1967
Laurence William Lane, Sr. at the age of thirty-eight when he bought Sunset Magazine.

letting an advertiser know that SUNSET was not to be pushed around.

I remember his frustration at advertisers' slowness to recognize SUNSET. We both enjoyed making up a dummy of a SUNSET without advertising.

Larry would never forgive me if I failed to mention our goldfish and waffle irons. Our advice on how to kill algae in a goldfish pool also killed some goldfish. The expensive kind seemed especially sensitive. Larry paid for quite a few goldfish. But it certainly was proof of reader action and SUNSET's responsibility. The waffle iron incident was the result of advising that you could make your waffle iron clean as new by filling it with salt and leaving it turned on for 3 to 6 hours. The only trouble was that the irons melted. Larry cheerfully signed waffle iron checks for a month

without seeing an iron. The next month we slowed down the checks by asking the readers to send us the damaged irons.

I remember when SUNSET was teetering, issue by issue, between black and red ink, Larry turning down a 12-page contract because it called for editorial support. (Ironically the type of editorial called for was scheduled for future issues.) Larry really welcomed this opportunity to show SUNSET's muscle. To him the money lost was an investment.

I remember a letter to Larry from the editor whom I had succeeded saying something about Doty editing SUNSET with a hoe and a hammer. At the time I thought —and by a publisher with a sledge and a whip.

Many will remember with me how Larry could cut through wishful or fuzzy thinking with such seemingly simple logic that he left you dumb and shaken. But at the same time he was willing to toss the wildest dreams back and forth with obvious pleasure.

I remember that the dream of moving SUNSET into the suburbs was an early dream. I remember an inquiring visit with Sam Morse at Hotel Del Monte about sites in Monterey for SUNSET. The site of the old capitol grounds was about right, but too far away. And the War Department took over Hotel Del Monte.

He was a fighter. He was tough. You couldn't stop him. But you could hurt him terribly by a thoughtless action or inconsiderate word.

I remember with awe his drive for perfection in everything he did—improving a spring, building a barn, building SUNSET. He was a perfectionist. But I remember him most fondly as one with great tolerance for imperfections in those who worked with him—like me.

Walter T. Doty

Stet marks the passing of Laurence Lane with a tribute written by Walter Doty, March 3, 1967.

One thing my dad taught me was that publishing is a three-legged stool: you have to start off with appealing editorial content, then circulation— *Sunset* made a profit off subscriptions and newsstand sales, one of the few magazines to do so—and then advertising, making money on the first two. As *Sunset*'s publisher, I was personally involved in all three activities.

The magazine's circulation kept rising, in part because of the growing population of the West, but also because of the further expansion of *Sunset* territory. In June 1968, Alaska was added to *Sunset*'s editorial territory, although the magazine had long reported on it as a travel destination. In March 1971, the magazine's circulation reached 1,000,000, and the April issue was the first to carry more than $1 million worth of advertising. In April 1977, *Sunset* added the four Rocky Mountain states of Montana, Wyoming, Colorado, and New Mexico to its circulation and editorial territory. A decade later, *Sunset* had more than 1.4 million subscribers, and our four regional editions were read by an estimated five million men and women. At the time, we had 130 book titles in print, and Sunset Films, started in 1971, had produced more than eighty-five films and videotapes.

Meanwhile, *Sunset* continued to internationalize its coverage. As immigrants to California increasingly came from Mexico, Central America, and Asia, the magazine began incorporating Asian and Hispanic influences into its editorial content, with articles on everything from Japanese architecture to Mexican cuisine. In fact, nearly every issue carried material about Mexico, which was rapidly becoming a competitor with the Mediterranean countries as a Latin travel destination. The magazine rarely published an issue without reporting on one or more Pacific Ocean countries, and the book division kept a dozen books on the area constantly updated.

Sunset's coverage of food reflected this national influence and international orientation. Its emphasis on local products helped revolutionize American cuisine. *Sunset* helped assimilate asparagus, artichokes, eggplants, and avocados into American cooking. We picked up on some of the early pioneers who used fresh produce in cooking, brought them to our test kitchens, and had them work with our cooking editors. Also we introduced exotic fruits, such as mango, papaya, and kiwi. We established sourdough French bread as the bread of the West, we championed Jack cheese, and we put cilantro on the map. The list goes on and on. *Sunset* helped popularize the barbecue, a Spanish colonial practice conducive to the Western climate.

The increase in the size of the issues, the number of pages, brought in more and more advertising revenue. What we began to do was increase our cost per thousand: in other words, the amount we charged advertisers for running ads in *Sunset*. What we were getting was more revenue with fewer pages. We were able to capitalize on two-home ownership, two-car owner-

March 1979   95 cents

Sunset

The Magazine of Western Living

Inexpensive Add-ons
for Storage, for Living P. 94

"Come for Soup" Party P. 148

Long Beach Grand Prix P. 92

Which Power Tiller? P. 206

New Garden Book
Is Horticultural Event

ADVANCE SAMPLE
How to Plan Garden Color P. 76

Sunset, March 1979.

ship, and the popularity of four-wheel-drive vehicles in the West, especially in the early years of four-wheeling. I remember that at one point we carried more four-wheel-drive vehicle advertising in one issue than *Time*, *Newsweek*, and the *New Yorker* carried in the full year.

What you found when you went from the U.S. national audience to the Western audience to the *Sunset* reader was an increase in the frequency of purchase, or the volume of purchase, or the use of certain products. Cars were a case in point. In the late 1980s we were showing a significant percentage of *three*-car owners among our readers, which was just off the charts from the national pattern of ownership. We would send out letters to a hundred key auto dealers announcing a *Sunset* campaign and how the Western market had a higher percentage of two-car owners, and how *Sunset* had a higher percentage than the Western average.

Gardening continued to be one of the most highly read sections and one of *Sunset*'s distinguishing features, even though it was weak on advertising. We introduced the "Sunset Garden Preview" in 1950 as a way to tell Western nurserymen about wholesale sources for hard-to-get plants described in upcoming issues. Of all the advertising categories in Sunset, gardening was probably the one that received the greatest priority and attention, even though it was the smallest category. The gardening industry was very sensitive and critical when we would come out with a new plant material or a new technique, whatever it might be, that they hadn't been briefed on, and it would catch them off guard.

A good nursery—the specialists who know a hell of a lot about that flower, how to treat it, how to put the soil in, and so on—doesn't like to be caught off guard. We wanted to make allies of the garden trade industry, to show them that they were our partners and we were their partners, and we were working together to serve the public, and hopefully to help the industry grow. We would also share with the nursery the source of ordering the plant material. We'd work with the Armstrong nursery, for example, which actually had retail stores, too. Or the rose and bulb people up in the Northwest. When new varieties were coming along we would, in that garden preview, list the sources for ordering the new plant material. We would get very good cooperation, because the nurserymen wanted *Sunset* to be

Sunset, July 1976.

Sunset *The Magazine of Western Living* • *May 1978*

Monitoring *the progress of our birthday report, from left to right, are Bill Lane, Ken Cooperrider, and Proctor Mellquist*

Bill Lane and editors Proctor Mellquist (right) and Ken Cooperrider review draft pages from the forthcoming 80th anniversary issue of the magazine, in May 1978.

informed, as it was a conduit to probably many of the best gardeners here in the West—not all of them, by any means, but very near.

Here again, one could see the differences between the West and the rest. I remember we had a big article on gray plants that were to be used as an accent or a border plant and also when that red-and-green ornamental cabbage came along. We used to get skeptical comments from *Better Homes and Gardens* when we'd introduce this stuff. They just couldn't see that they could ever get any of the Eastern or Midwestern readers to take to it—although in fact a lot of what started in the West has had a considerable influence on the rest of the country.

I was certainly hands-on when it came to editorial, but definitely not heavy-handed. I was often asked whether I "approved" the magazine each month. I was always involved in the monthly meeting to decide on the cover. Usually I wanted people on the cover. I didn't like static scenes. As for what got printed between the covers, we had a strong policy book to guide the editors, and in any case I had a wonderful relationship with Proctor Mellquist and, beginning in 1980, his successor, Bill Marken. We knew what to expect from each another.

The editorial process we used at *Sunset* eliminated unpleasant surprises. If you went into *Sunset*'s offices, as you walked through the editorial department you would see an idea that I started: in order that everybody could look at what was coming up in the next issue, the entire issue was pinned up on the wall, starting with the first layouts. As the layouts evolved, anyone was welcome to suggest changes—a headline, for example, if they could think of something better. Any change you made you had to initial, so that somebody could follow up and ask you about it. A garden editor might have an idea for how to improve a food article, on the order of: "You know, I didn't get the connection between this and that. And if I didn't get it, maybe readers won't understand it. Maybe you ought to clear that up." That's what we called staff writing. It imposed a kind of collective quality control, and it proved to be extremely effective, month after month.

I myself would go past that board long before it was final, when it was up there in rough draft. Once in a while I might tell Mellquist or somebody, "I think that's a little off base for us." I remember they came up with an article on boutique breweries, which was quite a fashionable thing starting in the 1980s. I said, "It's fun, it's a good tourist attraction, but how can you promote editorial and come across credibly not only to readers but to advertisers when you don't accept beer advertising?" So we knocked it out. I remember there was one such brewery in the old downtown of Portland that they'd restored, and I said, "Well, okay, a paragraph or so in there, as one of the attractions to see." But that's quite different from a feature article on boutique breweries.

Much more significant than my input in particular issues of the magazine was my influence on its long-term editorial evolution, most importantly its growing environmental consciousness and advocacy. It was in this domain, that of the environment and conservation, that *Sunset* and its readers demonstrated an ability to adapt and to accept limits. This, too, it turns out, separated the West from the rest, with *Sunset* very definitely on the leading edge.

Bill Lane at the San Mateo County Horsemen's Association Ride in 1956.

Chapter 4

True West

On the Trail of John Muir

In 1922, Dad came out from Iowa and visited Lake Tahoe and Yosemite National Park with a group led by Edwin Meredith, the publisher of *Successful Farming*. Mr. Meredith had recently served as secretary of agriculture under President Woodrow Wilson, and in that same year, 1922, he founded *Better Homes and Gardens*. That trip was a turning point for Dad, who then wanted to show his family those world-famous destinations to prove that living "out West" was *really* different. So, Mel and I and Mom were raring to go when he planned a vacation for us during our first California summer, in 1929.

In San Francisco, we boarded the *Delta Queen* overnight ferry to Sacramento, drove to the Tahoe Tavern in our new air-cooled Franklin automobile, and eventually crossed over Tioga Pass into Yosemite Valley. Coming around the top of the lower valley, high on the north side, along the Old Big Oak Flat Road, and suddenly seeing Bridal Veil Falls on our right, El Capitan on our left, and Half Dome in the distance made a huge impression on two young kids from the flat farmlands of Iowa.

That childhood experience—the sudden view upon entering the valley—had a lifelong influence on both Mel and me, personally as well as on our professional and public service careers, as the concern for the natural environment began to get more attention, especially in the West, with its vast areas of open space.

A few years later, when we were teenagers, Dad arranged for us have summer jobs in Yosemite Park, where at one point I was a ticket taker on the valley tour buses. Mel also worked summers in Yosemite, and between us we spent some time at just about every job available to students in those years. I later talked myself into becoming an intern lecturer and found that I loved the educational challenge of meeting visitors from across the United States and abroad—even Japan and Germany—and talking about the history of the park. From the start, I learned to associate that history with the name of Abraham Lincoln.

Our family had—and continues to have—a special connection to Lincoln. Although I was born in Des Moines, Iowa, across the Mississippi River from Illinois, my father spent much of his youth on a farm in Moline, in northern Illinois. His mother, Grandma Lane, who lived to be ninety-seven, once told me that she had been held in her father's arms to watch President Lincoln's funeral train slowly pass by for his burial in Springfield. Fast-forward to my wife, Jean, who was born in Lincoln, Illinois, near Springfield. Also, her family has been very supportive of Lincoln College, in her hometown, which has a wonderful Lincoln Museum that is an outstanding complement to the amazing Lincoln National Museum and Library in Springfield.

Early on, I became fascinated with the connection between Lincoln and California. I learned that before he became president, Lincoln gave an increasingly high priority to California, beginning before the Gold Rush and especially once it became the thirty-fourth state, in 1850. As president, Lincoln signed a law in 1864 setting aside Yosemite Valley and the Mariposa Grove of Giant Sequoias to be protected from commercial development—or, in the words of the act, "to be held for public use, resort, and recreation, unalienable for all time." This was a first-of-its-kind decision by a national government in the world. Yosemite hadn't been "discovered" until about the mid-1850s, when the first white man saw it, so to get it designated as a protected area by 1864 was phenomenal.

The act of Congress was called the Yosemite Grant, even though it included the Mariposa Grove. Those two large, separated wilderness areas in the very remote High Sierras were placed under the jurisdiction of the State of California—and they are still regarded as the first *state* park by the Department of Parks and Recreation.

I remember sharing a personal feeling with President Richard Nixon, who appointed me chairman of the Commission on the Centennial of the National Parks in 1971, that the language of the act President Lincoln signed was tantamount to an "Emancipation Proclamation for the Environment"—a characterization I have repeated many times since. This was the first crucial step in saving the Yosemite Valley from excessive exploitation: entrusting it to the people of California.

This historic measure was a major factor leading to the national parks idea. Two decades later, the same spirit motivated the Congress and President Ulysses Grant to create Yellowstone National Park, on March 1, 1872. It was the first *official* national park. In taking this step—revolutionary in terms of recognizing the need to set aside and protect natural resources—

our country's leaders created a new park to be enjoyed by *all* the people, instead of by just the privileged few.

The national parks are the boldest environmental leadership step that the United States has ever taken, probably even until today. Granted, most countries just didn't have as much land available to set aside as we had in Western America after the Civil War. Yellowstone became a national park in 1872 because the government owned an enormous amount of land.

As a major commitment of national purpose, Yellowstone was what has been referred to as "the flowering of the idea." But Yosemite, which would achieve national park status in 1890, had established the precedent for federal protection of scenic wilderness, thanks to the farsightedness of President Lincoln, who had taken the crucial first step in 1864, in the midst of the Civil War.

Of course, we know that Lincoln did not live to see how others built on his achievement. During his last days, he told an old Illinois friend, "I have long desired to see California." He said he hoped to visit California after he returned from a post-presidential trip to Europe. My understanding is that he was really hoping to permanently retire in California and even travel to Alaska and Hawaii—although perhaps that's a bit of wishful thinking in hindsight on my part. In any case, it never had a chance to become a reality.

So Abraham Lincoln was one of my early "Western" heroes—and close on his heels came John Muir. One could argue that the modern environmental movement, with its various political and economic dimensions, really began in Yosemite with the early writings of that self-described vagabond Muir. Even though I had read in school about this remarkable and farsighted man, looking back on my school days I think far too little time was spent on his contributions to mankind.

John Muir's love of nature dominated his memories of his childhood in Scotland, where he was born in 1838. That same love of nature attracted him like a magnet to the woods and meadows surrounding his family's new home in Wisconsin, and drew him, in adult life, from Florida to Alaska, from Australia to South America. Yet in all his seventy-six years, spent traveling many thousands of miles, no one region claimed his heart as did the Yosemite Valley. When his sea voyage from New York to San Francisco ended, on March 28, 1868, he lost only three days before setting out on foot for the valley that was to become his "Sierra temple." He often called it "home," and it was indeed his first home in California.

Muir marked his thirtieth birthday during that first visit, and the valley gave him more inspiration for his great work than any other place. And just think about all the material he had to draw from! There are a score of natural wonders, easily visited, in today's Yosemite National

SUNSET

PUBLISHED MONTHLY AT SAN FRANCISCO
BY THE
SOUTHERN
PACIFIC
COMPANY

EDITED BY CHARLES SEDGWICK AIKEN

Vol. XI   JULY, 1903   No. 3

President Roosevelt in the High Sierra

His Stay of Four Days in the Yosemite Valley

By Carl E. Ackerman

> *"This is the one day of my life, and one that I will always remember with pleasure. Just think of where I was. Up there, amid the pines and silver firs, in the Sierran solitude, in a snowstorm, too, and without a tent, I passed one of the most pleasant nights of my life."*—President Roosevelt on the morning of his return from Glacier Point in the Yosemite Valley.

WHEN President Roosevelt reached the Yosemite valley on his recent trip through the west he was in a condition aptly described by a member of the party as "pumped out." For six weeks he had been moving over the country, running the gamut of reception committees, governors, mayors and the distinguished citizenship that manages to be seated on the platform. In each state through which he passed joyous school children had marched past him piping the national anthem, waving miniature "old glories" and shying an occasional soggy bouquet in his direction. Industrious committees, prideful of their country and its products, had bundled the illustrious guest, his Cabinet members and court, into carriages in which sat bebadged members of the county aristocracy and driven him over miles of country roads and paved streets. Other enthusiastic citizens at by-stations endeavored to show their appreciation of his passing in the midnight by firing revolvers and volleys of cheers in honor of the slumbering Chief Executive. With unexampled hospitality San Francisco had shown him that the sunlight that streams through the Golden Gate is not a circumstance to the warmth of its welcome to distingushed visitors.

So it was that when the President reached the valley he issued an ultimatum. He would view the wonderland in his own way and with but one companion, John Muir. And, leaving his party to enjoy themselves in their own

Sunset coverage of President Theodore Roosevelt's trip to Yosemite Valley in 1903.

From a photograph by Tibbitts.

THE DESCENT INTO THE VALLEY AFTER THREE DAYS' STAY IN THE MOUNTAINS

THIS IS OUR WEST

OUR WEST is many things; great things and little things which added together give us a different way of living.

Our West is a series of highways. Highways that stretch out to reach olives, peaches, sugar beets, grain; to find pears, flax, berries, apples, wheat; to challenge mountains; to explore forests; to wind alongside rivers; to climb past timberline into the snow; to hang a thousand feet above the ocean and sink to touch its sand.

Highways that wind across a patch-quilted valley floor, cut through an orchard of prunes, tunnel into a 10-mile lane of walnuts; turn, rise, and look upon the bay of San Francisco.

Though we work in offices, stores, factories, mills; though our address is a 10-story apartment house, we live on highways — for they bring life to us. Black, sleek pavements slicing through fields of lettuce, edging blue bays and acres of artichokes, sliding down avenues of palms and eucalyptus, looking down upon flat fields of beans and asparagus, crossing and recrossing 200,000 acres of oranges; quickly from mountain to seashore, from desert to desert.

WE LIVE at pavement's end: on trails; in the quiet peace of high mountains; along fish-filled lakes and rivers; through the green jungles of salal and vine maple in Olympic forests; pausing at the edge of a creek to pick red huckleberries. We float a fly on the Skykomish, a tapered line on Sierra lakes, a dry fly on the Mackenzie. We drag a sinkered spinner over the rocks of the Klamath, slowly reel in a deep-sunken fly on Lake Almanor.

Our West is many things. Yet, one thing is before us always—the fertile earth. We feel the slow deep-hidden rhythm of things growing. We see it pour forth in green growth, in flowers and in fruit. It is before us always. It travels with us on our highways. It returns with us into our homes and into our living, to absorb the tenseness—to quiet; to bring patience and contentment.

It is not the rhythm of stone and steel; of grinding gears and wheels, although they are everywhere. The nervous frenzy, the stretched-taut excitement of crowded people is not a part of it; for this is the West and its rhythm is of the earth—it is simple.

YET IT IS STRONG. It changes us, our thinking, our standards and values.

In the evening when the coals in the outdoor fireplace turn red and a wisp of blue smoke trails lazily through green branches, and dark green shadows pattern the fresh-trimmed lawn and there are but the small sounds of a late humming bird, or tired voices—then the basic rhythm of the West is our rhythm.

It flows through our hands when we bury them in the warm crumbly spring earth; in mixing soil for seed flats—two parts loam, one part peat, one part sand. It comes to us with the sight of the friendly wings of our own home; of red geraniums against an adobe wall; of old glass stained by the desert's sun; of a December rose; of our mountain cabin and the bunks we made.

This is our West!

From the pages of the January 1940 issue of *Sunset*.

The environmental awareness of the early *Sunset*, which reflected the Progressive Era's conservation ethos, is evident in such articles as "Sunshine as Power" in 1903 and "The Hetch Hetchy Problem" in 1909, both published under Southern Pacific ownership. These priorities continued from 1914 to 1929, when *Sunset* was a general-review magazine, in articles such as "How Long Will Our Gasoline Supply Last?"

Sunset under the Lanes continued this conservationist tradition, largely through the presentation of better ways of living. The magazine encouraged Westerners to appreciate beauty in both their homes and their travels, while emphasizing stewardship of the natural environment.

My father, I would say, was instinctively an environmentalist, and both Mom and Dad would have been in today's world. They followed a strict policy of no advocacy in *Sunset* magazine and books, however, to a degree that Mel and I, in taking the reins of the business, would feel the need to transcend that position in the face of mounting environmental challenges in the West. Ironically, my awakening to the need for real *environmentalism*, as opposed to conservationism, took place on the East Coast.

The place was Fire Island and the year was 1951. I was living in New York City, working as a salesman for *Sunset*. I was a bachelor, and I was asked by a gal that I was going with if I would go out and cook and make beds for four gals who wanted to play bridge all weekend on Fire Island. I was a big fan of the literary style and the fantastic writing of the *New Yorker*, and it just so happened that at that time the magazine was serializing Rachel Carson's *The Sea Around Us*, a book that had just been published. I brought along a collection of those issues to read on Fire Island. I would fix breakfast for these gals, make their beds, and fix them sandwiches, and then I'd go out on the beach to read. It was autumn and kind of chilly. I sat alone and read Carson's epic essay on the oceans in peril.

The Sea Around Us had a far-reaching influence on me in a lot of things I've been involved with in oceanography and population control over the years. I have referred to it in writing and in many talks. It certainly made me pay attention when her pathbreaking *Silent Spring* was published in 1962. I know it influenced my decision, several years later, to stop accepting DDT advertising for *Sunset*.

Another early influence was Aldo Leopold's book *Sand County Almanac*. Leopold, who is considered the father of wildlife management in the United States, was born in Burlington, Iowa, in 1887. An ecologist and forester, he was a pioneer in the development of modern environmental ethics. His *Sand County Almanac* contributed to the growing sense that man is part of an *ecosystem*, that everything is related. Leopold presented in scientific terms what John Muir had intuited and expressed half a century earlier in one of his most famous lines: "When we try to pick out anything by itself, we find it hitched to everything else in the universe."

Thanks to Carson and Leopold and others, "environment" was becoming a household word in the 1950s. The fact is, we were on the verge of an environmental revolution. And these pioneering publications were among the taproots of that revolution, which would lead to legislation on clean air and water, Earth Day, serious efforts at recycling, the reduction of pesticides, and the curbing of acid rain, as well as attempts to reverse global warming, save the remaining, dwindling rain forests, and improve land management along our coasts.

All of that still lay in the future when I returned to California from New York in 1952. But I already sensed the direction of things, and I wanted to do my part. In this spirit, one of the steps I took was to hire Martin Litton as *Sunset*'s travel editor in 1954. Litton later became a legendary Grand Canyon river runner and longtime environmental activist, best known as a staunch opponent of the construction of Glen Canyon Dam and other dams on the Colorado River. He made his first trip down the Colorado River through the Grand Canyon in 1955, thereby becoming the 185th recorded person to make this passage, which had been pioneered by the explorer and geologist John Wesley Powell.

Although his biggest environmental causes were still before him, at the time when I met Martin he had been writing controversial articles about Kings Canyon National Park and Dinosaur National Park for the *Los Angeles Times*. That got my attention and I decided to hire him. I vividly remember the interview in 1954. I was single. I had an apartment over on Waverly Street in Menlo Park. I never paid attention to the local trains, although I was living only about three blocks from the train tracks. But not Martin. All of a sudden he would look up and say, "That's a four-wheeler," or "That's a six-wheeler." I said, "What is?" He said, "That engine." He recognized the type of steam engine from the sound of it. He was a real train buff. I was a train buff too, and so we had a good interview.

I liked Martin's free spirit. He was also a pilot. He and I flew around a lot together. He had a Cessna 119, as I recall. I was learning to fly, and had always loved flying, although I never got my pilot's license. So we became very close friends.

Martin turned out to be a fantastic editor—one of the outstanding editors in the history of *Sunset*. And he was a fabulous writer and photographer as well. Before I hired him I read all of his controversial articles. I was reaching a point where I really wanted some fire in the belly in some *Sunset* articles that would have a strong environmental protection slant. I just made a decision. I wouldn't say my father opposed it, but he didn't lean that way. I was leaning very much that way when I came back from New York and became closely involved in *Sunset*'s editorial department in 1952.

Even had I not brought Martin on board, the environmentalists would have been bending my ear in order to try to influence *Sunset*'s coverage of, say, one or another Sierra Club issue. Usually I was somewhat at odds with the militant and, I felt, frequently inappropriate tactics of the environmental groups—such as sabotage and blockades—tactics about which they later became much more sophisticated. Anyway, Martin's roles as *Sunset*'s travel editor, on the one hand, and as environmental activist, on the other, were bound to come into conflict, and on occasion they did.

Martin was a kindred spirit and close friend of David Brower, who became the first executive director of the Sierra Club in 1952, the year he enlisted Martin in the campaign to oppose the construction of two dams in Dinosaur National Monument, on the border between Colorado and Utah. In 1956, Congress voted against approval for the dams. This was the beginning of Martin's long association with the Sierra Club and his unrelenting opposition to dam building on the Colorado. He was especially active in the struggle to prevent the construction of dams within Grand Canyon National Park.

I personally joined Martin in the Grand Canyon cause. In 1962, I was one of the first thousand recorded travelers down the Colorado in the Grand Canyon. I was with Martin in a double-ended boat, a dory we called the *Portola*. Martin, a contrarian by nature, stuck with the wooden dory even after most other river runners graduated to rubber rafts. That was before the Glen Canyon Dam created Lake Powell, and so we were on a lot of muddy water. In the end, the proposed Glen Canyon Dam was not defeated, but one of the reasons I went down the Colorado that summer with Martin was to try to block it. Here I was practicing what I preach, for I have long maintained that the best way to win these environmental battles is to get people to visit the site, so that they are better informed.

Dave Brower was someone I admired. I have always argued that in any important cause, you need crusaders and zealots who are not too compromising. If you want agreement by absolutely everybody or you want to placate your opponents, you frequently don't take the tough stand, make the difficult decision. So you need the Browers. He and I were good friends. I later helped him establish his Earth Island Institute.

As I say, it was through Brower that Martin became active in the Sierra Club during its more militant days, particularly in opposing the lumber companies. And in many ways, I shared their concerns and I supported their efforts. In 1960, *Sunset* ran a cover story titled "The Redwood Country," which is credited with launching a campaign that eventually led to

Sunset, October 1960.

the establishment of Redwood National Park. The park was established in 1968—ironically, the same year that Martin Litton and *Sunset* went their separate ways.

Martin was a difficult person, which I suppose he had to be in order to advance his causes. In fact, he could be very difficult. Proctor Mellquist was *Sunset*'s editor, but Martin was too big a figure for him to handle, so I ended up having to supervise him. He would use our stationery for completely unapproved correspondence to members of Congress. I remember once he wrote Governor Pat Brown in Sacramento a letter on our stationery, and Pat called me up and said, "Bill, what the hell is going on?"

One time Martin used my personal plane to fly over some forest up in Northern California at an illegal altitude, and I got a call from the FAA telling me that my plane was going to be grounded. I asked why and they told me, "Well, you were flying too low." I said, "I wasn't flying. I loaned it to a friend."

I finally had to give Martin the opportunity to retire. I never liked to fire anybody, and this was one of the few times I had to. It wasn't because I didn't admire him or because I disagreed with him. Really, I was very much sympathetic to his shock treatment tactics. I continued to support some things he did. And it wasn't his errant use of *Sunset*'s stationery or my airplane. The fact was, we were getting too many complaints from other members of the staff that he just wasn't playing by the rules.

Martin was always fighting with the editors on their editing of his copy. Sometimes I'd come in and change the opening lines on him; he would have a blatant arousal-type lead-in that I felt was just too strong, and it would editorialize, which was not our purpose. Although our bias was definitely pro-environment, we strived to present a balance of viewpoints on issues. Above all, our purpose was to inform. Let the readers decide—they're all intelligent, and a large percentage of them are college graduates.

We were a staff-written magazine. Our editors were all required to do a lot of good, solid single-column stories, with maybe one photograph to capture a reader's attention and give them a complete service. It's much tougher to do that than to spread photographs and all kinds of text over ten or twelve pages. Martin didn't like to do the little one-column stories;

he always wanted to do big cover stories, the kind of mega-articles we could only take about once or twice a year. For all those reasons, we decided he should retire. But we remained very good friends.

Blowing the Whistle

In the meantime, starting in the mid-1960s, Mel and I began to take active roles in a wide range of environmental efforts in our communities and at the state and federal levels, in both Republican and Democratic administrations. Mel was the first chairman of the San Francisco Bay Conservation and Development Commission and later the first chairman of the California Coastal Commission, both precedent-setting environmental agencies. I served, among other things, as chairman of a presidential commission charged with reviewing the National Park Service and making recommendations for its future development; and later I was the head of an advisory board for the California Desert Region administered by the Bureau of Land Management.

So Mel and I reached out, but *Sunset* was always our base. In the coming years we would host many meetings with business and environmental leaders at *Sunset* headquarters in Menlo Park. *Sunset* magazine and books were often the main media influence in the West for supporting good environmental causes. The magazine not only informed readers but often worked directly with the National Park Service, California State Parks, the Forest Service, the Sierra Club, the Save the Redwoods League, and other responsible organizations that were dealing with emerging environmental issues. *Sunset*'s influence on the national conversation was clear from the number of times readers wrote us to ask, "Can we buy reprints?"

The magazine was more and more in the public eye. In response to this, in May 1968 I initiated a new feature, "Letter from *Sunset*," a one-page editorial appearing at the back of the magazine. I felt we had to give the magazine an official voice. The column was usually written by the editorial staff, but sometimes I used the space to explain one or another feature in that particular issue of the magazine, and oftentimes I commented on Western developments that might especially interest or concern readers.

This new feature of the magazine was put in place just in time for the breakthrough developments of 1969, a turning-point year for the environment. A major catalyst was the Santa Barbara oil spill in January, which galvanized public opinion like nothing else. In the coming months, the National Environmental Policy Act established the President's Council on Environmental Quality; and the Environmental Protection Agency would follow within a year. Earth Day was established in 1969, and first celebrated the following April. There was suddenly an enormous amount of grass-roots activity and a lot happening with public interest groups and lawmakers.

Our concern with environment

The world in which Westerners live has been, is, and always will be of special concern to *Sunset*. For a dramatic example, see the article on page 58, in which we advise readers to stop using DDT and several other related insecticides in their gardens. We not only state why these insecticides shouldn't be used but also tell how to get rid of those you have, and recommend other controls to replace them.

For several years our garden editors and our management, reviewing evidence that DDT and related chemicals are extremely long-lasting pollutants, have been giving greater attention to other means of pest control.

On April 22, 1969, the daily press reported four biologists' discovery that brown pelicans on Anacapa Island, south of Ventura, California, this year had abnormally fragile eggs with heavy concentration of DDT in the yolks. Here was the first strong evidence of DDT's indirect damage to a species of life in the West. It lent great weight to the argument that the potential dangers of using DDT and certain other chlorinated hydrocarbons outweigh the advantages of using them. That same week we scheduled an article on the subject for this August issue, to allow plenty of time for our usual checking to make sure facts were straight and fairly stated.

On June 18 our publisher, L. W. Lane, Jr., with the full support of management and editorial staff, announced his decision that *Sunset* would no longer accept advertising for products containing DDT, DDD, aldrin, dieldrin, endrin, and heptachlor. *Sunset* has been carrying more such advertising than any other general consumer publication; but we could not reasonably continue to carry advertising pages extolling these products when our editorial pages recommended against their use.

Meanwhile the same controversy reflected in the daily press was coming into our office in the responses to 56 "checking copies" of the article. These went to biologists, ecologists, zoologists, entomologists, chemists, insecticide manufacturers and packagers, physicians, and home gardeners.

The effect of their comments was to reinforce our conviction—even while recognizing that some allegations are not yet proven—that DDT is insidious and that we should tell home gardeners so. They also helped us state with greater precision how and why the other chlorinated hydrocarbons are similarly suspect, though a few appear to deserve limited use until good substitutes are available.

Recent editions of the *Sunset Western Garden Book* and other *Sunset* books on gardening already suggest alternatives to the chlorinated hydrocarbon products, and their next editions will be revised to conform to this month's article.

WINDOW ON THE WEST: View from the tower

Motorists driving State Highway 79 through central Arizona can pause at this landmark to stretch, enjoy the remarkable view from the tower, and perhaps eat a picnic lunch nearby. The vista from the top of the tower takes in the Verde Valley, Mingus Mountain, the Mogollon Rim, and the colorful approaches to Oak Creek Canyon. The tower marks a roadside rest area beside the freeway near the turnoff to Montezuma Castle National Monument (see page 26), about 90 miles north of Phoenix and 45 miles south of Flagstaff.

R. WENKAM

Bill Lane's "Letter from *Sunset*" about DDT, from the August 1969 issue.

Sunset became part of that national conversation that year when we decided to stop carrying advertising for DDT. Rachel Carson's *Silent Spring* had sounded the alarm about pesticides in 1962. More recently, scientists reported that certain forms of wildlife—California brown pelicans, peregrine falcons, bald eagles, and Dungeness crabs, among others—had taken enough DDT into their systems to make many adults no longer capable of reproducing, thus threatening their species with extinction.

At *Sunset*, we felt it was time to act. In a press release of June 18, 1969, we announced that we would no longer accept advertising for products containing DDT and five other insecticides. This decision preceded the anticipated January 1, 1970, ban ordered by the State of California directive on only two insecticides: DDT and DDD. In the meantime, three other states—Arizona, Wisconsin, and Michigan—had passed or proposed legislation to control the use of DDT and related chemicals. We took note of all this in our press statement, which also announced that the magazine would publish a comprehensive report on the subject in its August issue.

That report, "It's Time to Blow the Whistle on DDT," written by our garden editor, Joe Williamson, was a landmark moment for *Sunset*. The DDT furor, we informed readers, had prompted us to conduct our own survey of the matter. On the basis of all the evidence, we believed we could no longer afford to debate the question while continuing to promote the use of DDT. We urged our readers to stop buying DDT and five of its close relatives (aldrin, DDD, dieldrin, endrin, and heptachlor) whose nondegradability posed a special hazard, and instead to use other, safer chemicals available on the store shelves.

The verdict was presented in our straightforward, no-nonsense style: "*Sunset* will no longer recommend garden use of DDT or any of these five; will no longer accept advertising for products containing them; will remove them from future printings of its garden books; and has stopped using them in its demonstration and test gardens." My "Letter from *Sunset*" in the back of that issue placed our decision in the context of our general concern for the environment.

The article itself was only two pages long, but these were among the most closely edited two pages in the history of the magazine. The step we took might seem obvious from today's perspective, but at the time it was a big deal. *Sunset* carried more insecticide and pest-control advertising for home gardening use than any other publication in the United States. In truth, there was not a whole lot of DDT advertising as a percentage of the total, but the risk was that we would annoy DDT advertisers, who might decide to pull their other products. And in fact, Standard Oil withdrew advertising for its Ortho line of lawn and garden products, which cost us a considerable amount of money.

We had anticipated a backlash from advertisers, so we were not surprised. And we were relieved by the general reaction to our decision, starting with our own readers. Senator Gaylord Nelson, a kind of guru of the environment in the U.S. Congress and one of the sponsors of Earth Day, put my letter to advertisers announcing our DDT decision into the *Congressional Record*. The *Wall Street Journal* featured our decision in its pages. These reactions only helped to emphasize that there was a groundswell of enthusiasm for "get-tough" action. Our decision gave a boost to arguments for tougher controls on pesticides by groups in several states and in Washington.

Not by coincidence—although much more quietly—it was at this time that *Sunset* gave a nudge to the idea of organic gardening. This was long before it became the trend in home vegetable gardens across America. In the May 1969 issue, we reported on the enthusiastic university students who were cultivating vegetables without the use of manufactured chemicals at the U.C. Santa Cruz Garden Project, a first-of-its-kind university laboratory.

DDT wasn't the first time we experienced a conflict between our environmental impulse and our quest for advertising dollars. When we supported the creation of the controversial Redwood National Park, we lost a lot of advertising from Georgia Pacific, and from the California Redwood Association, which was a marketing group for redwood as lumber, as well as from Simpson Logging. I knew we would lose that advertising when we endorsed the park. But I also believed that we would get it all back eventually, and we did.

In December 1969, *Sunset* decided to discontinue accepting two-wheel trail-vehicle advertising, a step I explained in a "Letter from *Sunset*" the following October: "We believe that the encroachment of trail bikes into natural areas should be strongly discouraged." We also began to apply even tougher controls on real estate and land development advertising. Yet none of this had the effect of inhibiting the magazine's growth. On the contrary, circulation reached one million in March 1971, and the April issue was the first to carry more than $1 million worth of advertising—sold through nine advertising offices throughout the United States.

This was also a time when I personally began to take a public role outside of *Sunset*—though, as Mel and I had agreed at the outset, always in synergy with it. I was more of an extrovert than my brother. I had studied acting in college, and I had taken public debate. In the selling end of the business I was out talking, and I was frequently invited to conferences or business meetings, and to speak to college classes and business schools. So performing on the public stage was a natural for me.

In that turning-point year of 1969 I delivered a speech at the thirteenth National Conference on the U.S. National Commission for UNESCO, which had the theme "Man and His Environment: A View Towards Survival." I served as the first program chairman for planning the conference, which took place at the St. Francis Hotel in San Francisco in November. I called my talk "A National Need: An Environmental Ethic." Much of what I had to say that day is still relevant to our world over four decades later.

Looking back at the text, I am struck by its dire tone. I spoke of "a total environmental crisis today," and warned: "We are playing a deadly game of environmental brinkmanship." The forces of economic progress, I pointed out, had "created a demand on open land and natural resources to feed the furnaces of our free-enterprise system. But in the drain we are placing on our own nature's bounty that makes it possible to be the 'best-heeled' nation and to help others, we are becoming environmental paupers ourselves." These were "inconvenient truths" already back then.

I reminded my audience that John Muir had set forth on his trek to Yosemite just over a century earlier, and asked them to imagine how far we had wandered off course. "Muir, in all his wisdom, could not have foreseen the compounding pressures of today—with a whole Ponderosa and Jeffrey pine forest in Southern California slowly dying from automobile and industrial smog; all life in a once-clear lake dying of pollution, and his sun-and-cloud-filled blue skies now mustard gray and poisonous."

The remedy, it seemed to me, was obvious: "We must evolve, accept, and enforce an 'environmental ethic' which will provide a national code of standards to enable us to make judgments between right and wrong and to give us guideposts for our industrial and group conduct." Here I invoked Aldo Leopold and his *Sand County Almanac*, published twenty years earlier. In his chapter called "The Land Ethic," Leopold wrote: "An ethic, ecologically, is a limitation of freedom of action in the struggle for existence. As an ethic, philosophically, it is a differentiation of social from anti-social conduct."

In the spirit of Leopold's book, I said, we had to develop an all-encompassing "environmental ethic," and I warned that there was no time to lose. "If we do not act immediately by a wide-ranging dedicated effort, we are building castles on a melting iceberg. Time is running out. Noble words and occasional accomplishments are not enough."

Sunset in the 1970s reflected this new environmentalism. It still stood for the pursuit of the good life, but now with an increasing sense of social responsibility. The conservation ethos that Mel and I inherited from our parents now blossomed into an environmental advocacy. We became very opinionated, but always the opinion was based on an emphasis in the article to get the reader to visit the place. *Sunset* expressed its *concern* to readers

Bill Lane (center), flanked by Mel Lane and Governor Ronald Reagan, during a Ranchos Visitadores Ride in May 1968. On the far right is Governor Paul Laxalt of Nevada; on the horse in the background is William P. Clark, Jr., the future national security advisor and secretary of the interior under President Reagan.

about one or another environmental issue, always being careful to provide thorough and balanced information about it. We did not proselytize, and so we never intimidated or alienated our readers. As a result, our influence on social and environmental matters increased through these years.

Another reason for *Sunset*'s success on the environmental front was that we adhered to our credo that effective environmental awareness begins at home. We addressed *regional* problems—those that we felt would have a direct impact on the West—with practical solutions. The magazine could sharpen its focus on local issues by frequently zoning articles in its four regional editions. Although costly, this zoning allowed us to offer close-to-home experiences to readers in our Northwest, Central West, Southern California, and Desert editorial territories. In 1977, in answer to long-expressed demand, the four increasingly important Rocky Mountain states of Montana, Wyoming, Colorado, and New Mexico became *Sunset* territory.

This was still the old how-to-do-it *Sunset*, but sometimes the emphasis changed: a little less wilderness travel and more close-in or urban recreation, fewer articles about new homes and vacation houses and more remodeling projects. We were pioneers in community action articles. We ran a long series of articles that featured examples of how, say, garden clubs got together with Lions Clubs to tackle local problems, such as litter, a problem frequently discussed in *Sunset*. How a row of old trees was saved, how an old schoolhouse was saved and made into a children's museum—we covered a lot of ground.

Of course no environmental issue was more important than water. When you're talking about exercising proper stewardship in the West, you're talking first and foremost about water. Water is the fundamental resource, from drinking to gardening and farming to generating energy, including air-conditioning. Beginning in 1969 under Governor Reagan, I was chairman of the People and Water Panel of the Governor's Conference on California's Changing Environment, so I got to study some of the problems in detail. Water is the constant environmental challenge for the West, and *Sunset* faced up to it. We published many articles about water conservation and the smart use of water, including drought-resistant plants and fire-resistant plant material, and there were thousands of requests for reprints of those articles.

For our seventy-fifth anniversary issue, in May 1973, we took as the theme "Can the West Grow Wisely and Well?" We invited environmentalists and eight Western governors to offer comments on the future of *Sunset* country. That same year delivered the oil shock, which produced long lines at gasoline stations and forced the magazine to make some quick adjustments. A cover and article about skiing scheduled for January 1974 were yanked off the line and other content substituted. For the time being, any articles that called for long-distance automobile drives were off limits.

Another *Sunset* reaction to the fuel shortage was a string of articles reporting homeowners' experiences with solar heating and cooling. Both *Sunset* magazine and books really ran with this, most notably in the *Sunset*

Sunset, February 1979.

Homeowner's Guide to Solar Heating, published in 1978. The February 1979 issue of the magazine featured reporting on solar heating, with a cover story on a Colorado home of singer-songwriter John Denver (although we had to agree not to identify the owner). The articles in this issue offered illustrated examples of solar-heated homes in New Mexico and Colorado. The following year, Pacific Gas & Electric collaborated with *Sunset* editors to construct a working model of solar technology open to the public at *Sunset*'s headquarters.

That February 1979 issue marked fifty years of Lane ownership of *Sunset*. Clearly, in the 1970s, without announcing it, *Sunset* enlarged its four editorial areas—home, gardening, travel, and cooking—to include a fifth: conservationism and environmental living.

History had shown that Westerners were willing not only to take more risks but also to change, to compromise, and to break with tradition. *Sunset*, I'd like to think, helped lead the way. Toward the end of the "environmental decade" of the 1970s, no less a champion of the West and of the environment than Wallace Stegner (another Iowan who became identified with the West) said it plainly: "*Sunset*, on its record, is as competent to deal with change as to reflect the unchanging."

But there was still a lot more work to do. As I wrote in my "Letter from *Sunset*" in the fiftieth anniversary Lane issue, "We are excited about the future but concerned that we stay down-to-earth and useful. Perhaps the biggest challenge for all of us will be to shift from a habit of plenty to a discipline of limits."

A Passion for Parks

The parks are a unique feature of the West. Some 80 percent of all the acreage of national parks is in the Western part of the United States. And if you take the National Forest Service, under the Department of Agriculture, something like 96 percent of all of the national parks and national forests that are open to the public are in Western America.

Sunset naturally had a tremendous involvement with national parks in the West, and here I played a high-profile role, especially when President

Bill Lane, circa 1975.

Nixon asked me to serve as chairman of the Centennial Commission on National Parks. Nixon knew of my background in the parks. I had had two appointments under President Johnson. One was on the Travel Advisory Committee to the Department of Commerce's United States Travel Service under Secretary Luther Hodges. Then I served on the Travel Advisory Board for the National Park Service under Secretary of Interior Stewart Udall. Nixon, who proved to be a strong environmentalist, gave tremendous support to the National Park Service, that wonderful institution, and to the celebration of the centennial of national parks.

Chairing the Centennial Commission was a big job. I moved to Washington, but it was rather late in the planning, in the fall of 1971, because there had been some politics involving the four members of the Senate and the four members of the House—each body represented by two Democrats and two Republicans—about where the chairmanship should go: to one of them, or to the private sector. They finally decided to tap someone from the private sector, and I got the call.

The theme of the centennial was "Parks, Man, and His Environment," to remind us all of the interrelationships between the preservation of natural and other resources by national parks and, equally important, their dependence on the wise actions of man as the custodian of our environment. Yellowstone came first, and almost a century later, with thirty-five more national parks and more than two hundred other facilities administered by the National Park Service, we were preparing to celebrate the Centennial of Yellowstone and the system of parks that came after it. By "national parks" we meant landmarks as varied as the Grand Canyon and Independence Hall—each of which belonged to all the citizens of the United States.

In my opening remarks at the National Park Service press meeting, in November 1971, I decided to use the opportunity to set the tone for the commission. My point from the beginning was that the centennial had to be a lot more than a birthday party, that we had to take it as a platform to look ahead and to establish an agenda for the next century. Not that that was such a monumental point of view, but nobody had really focused on it.

In making the case for the parks, inevitably I invoked Muir, quoting some of his best-known lines from 1898: "Thousands of tired, nerve-shaken, over-civilized people are beginning to find out that going to the mountains is going home; that wildness is a necessity; and that mountain parks and reservations are useful, not only as fountains of timber and irrigating rivers, but as fountains of life."

I warned that the road ahead would not be easy in achieving the ideal goals for our national parks, but that one thing was certain: it could be accomplished only if we as a country were "objective, bipartisan and courageous in setting idealistic goals and working together to achieve them" into the next century. "If we can achieve as much for our successors to enjoy in the next hundred years of National Parks as our ancestors provided for us during the past hundred years, we will have achieved a large measure of success. Hopefully, we can do more!"

I presented what I felt was a kind of mission statement. Copies of my remarks were sent to all members of Congress, the entire staff at the White House, and all the superintendents from the National Park Service. The idea was to get everybody together on it. But it was late in the game, because the centennial of Yellowstone was in 1972, and we had to raise money, matching funds, in order to get the money appropriated by Congress. Richard P. Mellon was on the committee, and he gave a gift, and I gave a gift, and with that as a foundation, we were able to raise the amount of money necessary to qualify for the congressional appropriation. Only then could we begin to get the centennial programs under way.

We had a number of celebrations. We had a big environmental conference in Yosemite, an international conference in Yellowstone, and a presidential conference for national park leaders in Washington. We had seminars where we brought in all kinds of park officials from county and city parks. We produced medallions and postage stamps. We did all kinds of things. It was a massive undertaking. And it lasted for the full year of 1972.

I wasn't able to remain in Washington for the entire year, for reasons having to do with the call of family and the pressures of *Sunset*. I resigned the chairmanship in the middle of 1972, remaining on board as a consultant. By then we had raised all the funds, and the entire program was set in place and had been approved by Secretary Rogers Morton. In my place, Edmund B. Thornton, of Illinois, came in and did a good job of following through. But I had the satisfaction of knowing that I had gotten the show up and running.

I returned to *Sunset*, which devoted coverage to the centennial and looked ahead "Into the Second Park Century," in the title of one "Letter from *Sunset*." In January 1973, a *Sunset* editorial titled "That Grand Mountain Park for Los Angeles" gave favorable attention and encouragement to a bold scheme for the Santa Monica Mountains. This and numerous reports in *Sunset* helped bring an eventual victory in November 1978, when President Jimmy Carter signed a law establishing the Santa Monica Mountains National Recreation Area.

I have already mentioned *Sunset*'s role in advocating the Redwood National Park in the 1960s. Later we moved from advocacy to diplomacy to help deal with some of the problems that arose *after* the park was created. Many people associated with the timber industry opposed the creation of a park, and logging operations on adjacent private lands continued un-abated—and perhaps even accelerated—once the park was established. As a result, as much as 90 percent of the watershed of Redwood Creek was clear-cut. We were forcefully reminded of the words of Wallace Stegner, in his 1960 *Wilderness Letter*: "Something will have gone out of us as a people if we ever let the remaining wilderness be destroyed."

No sooner had the Redwood National Park been established than ef-forts got under way to enlarge the park in order to incorporate vulnerable stands of redwood forest. But there was disagreement among the various parties about where to draw the enlarged boundaries. A kind of bastard boundary had been hammered out for the park when it was created in 1968. Now the challenge was to fill in the gaps in order to round it out. The Sierra Club and the Save the Redwoods League couldn't agree on the new boundaries. What we did in *Sunset* was to publish an article giving both views and maintaining that there had to be a resolution. The idea was that we had to work out a compromise between the Sierra Club and the Save the Redwoods League.

Mel and I hosted a lunch at *Sunset* with representatives from both groups. Nathaniel P. Reed, assistant secretary of the interior for fish and wildlife and parks, came out from Washington. Also we had representatives of the three big logging companies operating in redwood country come down to *Sunset*. It was a full day of group and one-on-one meetings, and it helped break the logjam. In 1978, Redwood National Park expanded, add-ing 48,000 acres to the original 58,000. In the meantime, some of the virgin timber and some of the watersheds had been cut, but at least the agreement rescued a part of it.

My connection to Washington continued when President Nixon ap-pointed me to the secretary of the interior's Advisory Board and Council on National Parks. I served on this panel under four presidents: Nixon, Ford, Carter, and Reagan. It was fun, although it was always very demanding. There was hardly an issue in the national park system that was not put be-fore the secretary's advisory board. There were lots of subcommittees, and it was really a no-holds-barred situation, in the sense that the board could take the initiative in the areas it wished to study. I spent quite a bit of time in Washington, sometimes staying a couple of weeks at a time. I'd fly home on weekends, and maybe catch the Monday-morning executive committee meeting at *Sunset*, then fly out again on the red-eye Monday night.

Only this kind of firsthand experience allows you to see how truly dif-ficult it is to get things done—on the environment or most anything—in government, especially in Washington. That's one reason I have so much admiration for William Mott, who served under Ronald Reagan both in

Sacramento and in Washington. Bill and I were friends and occasional collaborators. As governor, Reagan appointed Bill director of the California Department of Parks and Recreation, a position he held during both Reagan terms, from 1967 to 1974. It is a credit to Bill's diplomatic skills and his sheer tenacity that during his tenure the state park system added 154,000 acres to the existing 800,000 acres. What an achievement!

Bill Mott then stepped onto the national stage when President Reagan appointed him director of the National Park Service, a position he held from 1985 to 1989. It is fair to say that park officials had been demoralized by the policies of Interior Secretary James Watt in the first Reagan term, so there was great excitement when Bill Mott's appointment was announced. I myself got so excited that I asked Attorney General Ed Meese's permission to have Bill sworn in at *Sunset* headquarters. Meese gave his approval.

The ceremony took place on May 17, 1985, with a lunch at *Sunset*. There was a second ceremony held on federal government property—at the U.S. Geological Survey, down the street in Menlo Park—just to make it fully legal. About a week later, he was sworn in again in Washington, but in the meantime he was able to get the ball rolling and issue his famous "Twelve Point Plan," designed to protect the parks, to better serve the public, and to improve the management of the Park Service.

When Bill Mott returned to the Bay Area in 1989, it was as a special assistant to the National Park Service. He was tasked with planning the conversion of the historic Presidio at San Francisco from a military base to a National Park Service site. Spanish explorer Juan Bautista de Anza founded the Presidio in 1776 to guard the Golden Gate. In 1853, the U.S. military razed the Spanish fort and constructed a three-tiered, brick-and-masonry Fort Point. In 1988 the military declared the 1,400-acre Presidio—the oldest continuously active army post in the nation—obsolete. It was scheduled to be closed—but it could not be sold, thanks to legislation passed by Congress in 1972 creating the Golden Gate National Recreation Area, or GGNRA. The arrangement assigned the National Park Service to administer Fort Point and waterfront areas of the post.

For the Park Service the Presidio was a dream inheritance, the environmental opportunity of a lifetime. The takeover was a big project that brought with it enormous complications and challenges—among them a lack of funds, local pressure for local uses, and national pressure for special uses—but Bill Mott was easily up to the task. "You can't win by just piddling along with the minor stuff," Bill liked to say. "You've got to think big."

Well, it just so happened that I was thinking along the same lines for *Sunset*. I, too, had just left the Reagan administration, after four years as ambassador to Australia. I came back in the spring of 1989. Normally our

THE MAGAZINE OF WESTERN LIVING

Sunset

NOVEMBER 1989 $1.95

THE HISTORIC PRESIDIO
Another Great Park for San Francisco? P. 78

A Really American Thanksgiving P. 168

Good Neighbor Remodels P. 96

Sunset and the Environment P. 230

Sunset, November 1989.

cover stories were a year or so in the making, but after Bill and I got together, I decided that I would change signals with the cover story, something I had never done before on such short notice. I no longer remember what the cover story was going to be, but the Presidio topic was so timely, and the politics of it were becoming so contested, that I couldn't resist.

I took one of our best editors, Dave Hartley, who lived in San Francisco, and in two months, working around the clock, we did a fantastic article on the Presidio, explaining its history, its possible future as a public park, and ways for readers to enjoy its staggering scenery. I had to pull a lot of strings to get some of the photographs and other access, but Bill Mott was very much with me, and so we cut through a lot of red tape. We produced an elaborate fold-out color-coded map—unlike anything done before—and gave it to the Park Service. The issue was a bang-up success. The Park Service sent it to every member of Congress. And we had a wonderful reaction from the army.

I decided to use the occasion of this special issue of the magazine to take stock of *Sunset*'s environmental agenda, in a signed editorial under the title "*Sunset* and the Environment: Working with You to Help Conserve and Improve the West." I expressed pride in the magazine's "strong, sometimes even fierce, commitment to protecting the quality of the environment in the American West." Here I drew the explicit comparison between *Sunset*'s purpose and methods and those of John Muir: "Muir won his converts by taking influential editors, politicians, and businessmen to Yosemite, identifying the issues, and making a strong case for the environment. *Sunset* tries to accomplish the same thing by showing 5 million readers—Western taxpayers and voters—how to visit an area, and encouraging them to get involved in its environmental questions."

If John Muir was the man, Yosemite National Park was—for the Lane family and for the entire *Sunset* staff—the symbol of the greatness that the national parks and the West have to offer. The Yosemite centennial proved to be the occasion for the final blockbuster issue of *Sunset* magazine under Lane ownership, in May 1990. All the focus of attention up to then, from the point of view of conservation, had been on what was happening on the floor of Yosemite Valley. Our cover article told readers how to visit the backcountry, where 90 percent of the acreage in Yosemite is wilderness area. Our purpose was to get people into the Yosemite backcountry and let them see it for themselves. Judging from the reactions we got from readers, legislators, and park officials, the issue was a success.

My close ties to the parks continued well beyond my *Sunset* years. I was very proud to be able to wear the hat of *both* an honorary national park ranger and an honorary state park ranger—a rare combination.

In 1994 I received the Conrad Wirth Environmental Award. Conrad Wirth was the longest-serving director of the National Park Service, from 1951 to 1964. Each year the National Park Foundation honors an individual for a lifetime of service. The ceremony at the White House included President and First Lady Bill and Hillary Clinton, and Secretary of Interior Bruce Babbitt, the former governor of Arizona. The thing that pleased me the most was that the announcement of my award coincided with President Clinton's announcement of the first annual National Park Week. That was something I had been lobbying for for years, so the timing of the announcement was especially satisfying.

In 1995, the National Parks and Conservation Association bestowed on me its highest honor, the William Penn Mott Jr. Park Leadership Award, named for my good friend, who passed away in 1992.

The sale of *Sunset* in 1990 allowed me to pursue a more vigorous philanthropic agenda related to parks and the environment. Over the years, and especially as I crossed the threshold into my ninth decade, I was inspired time and again by a passage from Rachel Carson's *The Sense of Wonder*, which she was writing at the time of her death in 1964. "Those that live with the mysteries of earth, sea, and sky, are never alone or weary of life," she wrote. "Every child should be endowed with a sense of wonder so indestructible that it would last throughout life."

Ambassador Bill Lane rides in the Royal Agricultural Society Easter Show in Sydney, March 1989.

Chapter 5

Ambassador Bill

Danger . . . and Opportunity

During my wartime service in the navy, a hell of a row broke out on board the ship between the navy gun crew and the communications crew. It fell to me, as one of the communications crew, to negotiate a truce. I argued to the men that here we were, in the middle of the ocean, where our lives depended on our efficiency and that meant our joint action: we had to rely on each other. There was no way around that fact. I finally got the two crews together, and within a short time we were all back working together, and in fact more effectively than before.

That little episode is emblematic of one of the threads that run through my entire life: getting people to cooperate. I've certainly had a considerable amount of practice. Although I had to decline a lot of appointments over the years, I've done more than my fair share of serving as chairman of one or another committee or board. The fact is, I like chairing meetings. I like organizing, setting goals and objectives. I like the process of getting people to work together, finding different people to tackle different assignments. And I just like the organizational structure of committees and groups and the challenge of making sure they function efficiently. I would guess that my reputation on all the boards on which I served was one of constantly kicking them in the butt to think differently or to think big, to throw the book out the window. One of the things I especially liked about being a United States ambassador was the challenge of working with diverse groups that all have their hierarchies going right into the U.S. Congress, where they lobby for funding and personnel promotions and on behalf of different and often competing policies. Getting those rival bureaucracies to work together in an embassy is something I just found to be a considerable challenge and a rewarding one.

I would say that I had a bent for leadership and diplomacy from an early age. Diplomacy is, after all, a form of selling, of persuasion, and I have always been a natural salesman and a pretty good communicator. I was president of my grammar school student body and then president of my high school student body. In May 1938, during my senior year at Palo Alto High School, I presided at the meeting of the junior organization of the Red Cross during the national convention of the Red Cross, held in San Francisco that year. Had I stayed on at Pomona College and not transferred to Stanford after my sophomore year, I might have become president of that student body as well, because I was the first freshman elected president of the fraternity at Pomona. At Stanford I chose not to pursue politics. Instead, I joined the undergraduate magazine, *Chaparral*, and became the first junior ever appointed its general manager.

After the war, my leadership of *Sunset* magazine served as a catalyst for getting me involved in public service. This was a natural fit, because *Sunset* was so heavily involved in issues of vital relevance to Western living, and also because the magazine encouraged its readers to take a personal interest in their local communities, at least to the extent of being informed about issues concerning growth, the environment, conservation, and preservation. I always insisted that there be a *synergy* between my public service and my stewardship of *Sunset*. It was a small company, and I just didn't feel comfortable going to Sacramento or Washington or anywhere in the world if the undertaking didn't reinforce what I felt could make me do a better job at *Sunset*.

A case in point was when President Richard Nixon appointed me to his National Advisory Committee on Oceans and Atmosphere, under the Department of Commerce, during his first term as president in the early 1970s. One of the presentations we had back in Washington was by specialists from a tree-ring research facility based in Flagstaff, Arizona. This was in a period when we were having shortages of rainfall that in the West turned into drought. These experts pointed out that tree-ring research, which allowed us to look back in time many hundreds of years, indicated that there had been numerous droughts that lasted for ten, fifteen, twenty, even thirty years.

I found this fascinating and I thought it would be of special interest to our Western readers. So I sent our executive editor, Ken Cooperrider, down to Flagstaff to visit this tree-ring research facility. This was a time when *Sunset* had become increasingly focused on environmental issues generally and on water issues in particular. The magazine took the position that we in the West just had to get smarter about the way we used our water. Cooperrider's trip to Flagstaff led to a very informative article in *Sunset* in October 1977, in the midst of one of the worst droughts in the West in a century. It placed that drought in historical perspective and, among other things, gave us reason to be optimistic about our dry spell coming to an end in the near future. That article only happened because of my access to that information about this tree-ring research when I was in that government agency in Washington.

About that same time I was moving very fast up the ladder of PATA, the Pacific Area Travel Association, an organization I had helped found back in 1951. Secretary of Commerce Luther Hodges appointed me secretary of PATA in 1980–81 under President Jimmy Carter. Here is a prime example, going back to my early years on the magazine, of the synergy between my devotion to *Sunset* and my attraction to public service. Mel and I both realized that the PATA region was bound to grow and be a source of advertisement revenues for *Sunset*. We hooked our wagon to PATA, as PATA did to *Sunset*. At an annual PATA convention in Honolulu, in March 1953, I gave the keynote speech, titled "Challenge in the Pacific." I was at the time sales manager of *Sunset* and I was very mindful of how PATA could be used to serve *Sunset* readers. My speech was part inspirational, part promotional, and mostly instructional. It was certainly full of solid ideas on what the traveling public—*Sunset* readers in particular—wanted in the way of information and promotion, and how PATA could serve a valuable role in providing it for them.

That speech of mine seemed to strike a chord. That same year, PATA's vice president of publications, Frederic Rea, former *Pacific Travel News* publisher on loan from *Sunset*, co-authored PATA's first major promotional piece, the *Pacific Travel Handbook*. The handbook, which detailed travel information on member countries, was distributed to travel agents and travel-related organizations. PATA went on to create international awareness of the Pacific region by producing a series of informative and up-to-date publications. Contributing to the success of those early publication efforts was the friendship between PATA and the Lane family, a relationship that grew stronger over the years.

That PATA convention marked the beginning of my outspoken advocacy of tourism for the West, and California first and foremost. During Governor Pat Brown's second term in office, in the mid-1960s, he appointed me to his Tourism Commission. Later, Governor Ronald Reagan reappointed me and named me chairman of the commission. Once on board, I immediately turned the focus to how tourism was a major money tree for California's economy. This may seem like an obvious point, but despite what our research at *Sunset* magazine demonstrated, tourism was at that time not considered a major producer of gross income or jobs or as a tax base. I went to my friend Bill Mott, who was the director of state parks at the time. We got some fast-track figures with entry-gate interviews of state park visitors, as well as follow-up questionnaires, plus figures from merchants and countless businesses, such as construction and insurance companies, that had never even considered that they were beneficiaries of tourism. Within a decade we had tourism close to the top among the recognized income producers and employers in the state, ranking with manufacturing, housing, and agriculture.

My preaching on the economic benefits of tourism brought in many invitations to speak on the subject. One talk I gave in 1969, when I addressed the Pacific Northwest Trade Association, was based on *Sunset*-paid research following the big oil spill in Santa Barbara that year. I gave it the title "The Day the Tourists Stopped Coming," although of course the talk was about the steps we ought to take to ensure that they never stopped coming. In the same way, a talk I gave in 1972 called "Is Hawaii Breaking Its Promise?" was geared toward encouraging Hawaii to live up to its potential as a major tourist destination.

The following year, 1973, brought the war in the Middle East and the OPEC oil embargo, which drove up fuel prices and seemed to threaten not only our economic well-being but our way of life. At the time of the oil crisis, and no doubt as a consequence of it, the State of Hawaii decided to cancel its advertising in *Sunset*. I screamed bloody murder to our salespeople back there: "Tell them that they've got the opportunity of a lifetime, with public transportation the only way you can get there from the mainland! Private boating may be cut, but how many people go over to Hawaii in a private boat?"

Some legislator over there was told of my remarks and he reported them to Hawaii's governor, John Burns. The next thing I knew, I had a call from Governor Burns asking me if I would come and address Hawaii's legislators on the subject, and naturally I accepted his invitation. Many of those legislators were Asian, of course. One of them, a lawmaker of Chinese descent, came up to me afterwards and said, "Mr. Lane, do you know that in Chinese we don't have a single character for the word 'crisis'? We say it instead with two characters, one representing 'danger' and the other 'opportunity.'" This was at a time when the word "crisis" was dominating the headlines. I said, "Will you scribble that out for me?" He did, and I verified it with the Chinese consulate in San Francisco (China at the time officially being Taiwan, of course).

I got so enthusiastic about this, amid all this talk of doom and gloom, that I paid for a full-page newspaper advertisement that appeared in the *Wall Street Journal* and numerous other daily newspapers. I wrote the ad a few weeks later, on a Pacific Southwest Airlines flight coming up from a meeting of Governor Reagan's Economic Development Commission in San

Diego. Most commission members delivered despairing reports on the energy shortage, inflation, and so on. I could have added to the hard-luck stories, but I didn't. The experience convinced me to make use of the Chinese characters for "danger" and "opportunity." The ad really took off.

We blew the ad up into a large poster and had thousands of reprints made. I would still see those reprints for years afterwards when I was active at *Sunset*, most often in an advertising office. There was even an office at the White House that had it posted. I later learned that President Kennedy had once used this crisis/opportunity formulation in a speech on foreign policy, but a decade after that, few people remembered it.

Out of danger comes opportunity. That philosophy had been my reaction to the oil crisis from the beginning. It was essentially our corporate philosophy at *Sunset* through depression, war, and other crises. That sense of optimism was an example set by my dad, who saw an opportunity for *Sunset* during the Depression, at a time when a lot of other magazines were not doing well and quite a few did not survive. In response to the oil shock, I encouraged our *Sunset* editors to highlight hiking, bicycling, and energy conservation, and to provide more coverage of public transportation.

I look back at the ad now and I see that the message is as relevant to our era of global warming and the challenges and opportunities it presents for innovative solutions, including new green technologies. "We know we have been living on borrowed time where energy is concerned," I wrote. "We know that our life-styles and our productivity may be altered drastically in the near term future. But we also know that shortages will force us to seek new answers, and, if we but look at the successive crises in our past, we can feel confident that solutions will be found. Another crisis, another opportunity. The way it so often happens." That remains the only way forward today, it seems clear to me.

I was motivated to write those lines by a very keen sense of patriotism, and yet the ad was unmistakably a *Sunset* ad. In the version we published in the *Detroit Free Press*, we devoted a special sidebar of text "To our friends in the auto industry," which included a series of charts showing the West's dependence on the automobile. It quoted my February 1974 "Letter from Sunset" editorial: "We continue to assume that the family car will play an important part in our readers' lives, and that they will find ways to use their cars more efficiently." Farther along, the ad copy drives the message home: "In this time of uncertainty and rising costs, advertisers have the opportunity to concentrate on a market where the pioneering spirit—the ability to adapt and roll with the punch—is its great strength. . . . The market is Western America. The access to its most stable consumers is through Sunset Magazine."

I have said all along that problems always create a demand for thoughtful explanations and helpful solutions. That's prime territory for magazines. *Sunset*, with its how-to-do-it format, was typically on the cutting edge.

World's Fair

I have never let political partisanship influence my public service. I have served on both sides of the aisle, as they say, whether in Sacramento or Washington. In Sacramento I had a lot of contact with the governor when I served on gubernatorial committees. In fact, I wouldn't take a job unless I had a commitment that I had access to the governor. I've had government responsibilities that were not directly the result of a chief executive's appointment, but whenever there was a gubernatorial appointment or a presidential appointment I always required a personal meeting with the governor or the president and an understanding that he would give the project his support.

I always brought it back to what it would do to help me with *Sunset*. I was always looking to broaden our base at *Sunset*, and of course I wanted to pursue my own interests in foreign affairs, foreign trade, and the environment, and all these things kind of all flowed together. Under both Governor Reagan and Governor Jerry Brown I was chairman of the Foreign Trade Subcommittee of the Commission for Economic Development. It was rather unusual for a person who was not in industry but coming out of publishing to be made chairman of a foreign trade committee. That appointment came about because I had some credentials on trade. I had been, through *Sunset*, working with the trade committee for the Chamber of Commerce in San Francisco, and a lot of the city's trade was with the Pacific. Looking back on it, I would say that that appointment to the Foreign Trade Subcommittee was a big stepping-stone to my becoming more deeply informed about national and international issues and more involved in public service.

I stepped up to the national stage when President Nixon named me chairman of the National Parks Centennial Commission in 1971, a story I recounted in the previous chapter. That centennial appointment led to an opportunity for me to get involved in the U.S. bicentennial celebration. In fact, I was asked by President Nixon to be chairman of the United States Bicentennial Commission. That was in 1972, leading up to the bicentennial in 1976. There had been several attempts, going back to the 1960s, to get the bicentennial organization off the ground—maybe back to the Eisenhower era. With only a few years to go, Congress finally bit the bullet and decided to create a government commission to organize the bicentennial.

At that point, Anne Armstrong, counselor to the president, asked me to come over to the White House and talk to the president. It turned out that the question was whether I would agree to be chairman of this new government commission, called the American Revolution Bicentennial Administration. I had to say no, mostly because of the long commitment involved. The job would extend well beyond 1976, because I would then have had to make a report to Congress on the accomplishments of the bicentennial, and I figured that that would take at least another two years. That was just too long a time frame for *Sunset* and for my family, and it was going to be a very, very heavy job to do from the West Coast. There are figurehead jobs and there are hardworking jobs, and this was going to be a hardworking job, with lots of commuting from California. I would practically have had to resign and live back in Washington.

So I declined that opportunity, but the conversation about the bicentennial ended up leading to other things. Henry Kissinger had been aware of my background and interests when he was with Nixon in the White House. As President Gerald Ford's secretary of state, Kissinger asked me if I would help coordinate the activities of the Pacific countries that were going to be participating in our bicentennial. This I agreed to do.

Beginning in early 1975, I traveled all over the Pacific, helping to facilitate the international dimension of our bicentennial celebration. Jean and I spent our twentieth wedding anniversary that April on Heron Island, on the Great Barrier Reef. I was down there to speak to a large business conference at the Opera House in Sydney, and to meet with the head of IBM in Australia, a man who was serving as chairman of the U.S. Bicentennial Committee for Australia.

The Australians had all kinds of things they were doing for our bicentennial. They gave a million dollars to Harvard for an endowed chair in Australian studies—a million-dollar donation that would be the equivalent today of $20 million. Malcolm Fraser, who was then prime minister and later became a good friend of mine, hand-delivered this million-dollar check to President Ford as one of Australia's gifts. The emperor of Japan gave a fabulous collection of bonsai, which is still in the Smithsonian National Arboretum. All the Pacific countries made contributions to recognizing our bicentennial, and my job was to help coordinate, suggest ideas, and foster cooperation. If I found a snag, say in the Philippines, where they weren't getting the right contacts in the United States, I would troubleshoot that and report to John Warner, the chairman of the American Revolution Bicentennial Administration, and to Kissinger, who was acting as a kind of overlord of the bicentennial.

This roving diplomatic work then led to my appointment as ambassador-at-large and commissioner general for the World's International Ocean Exposition on Okinawa, Japan, in 1975. The idea for that world's fair originated in the landmark visit that Nixon and Kissinger made to China in February 1972 as part of detente. Stopping in Tokyo on the way back, they signed an agreement with the Japanese government for the release of the Ryukyu Islands, which the United States had retained as part of the treaty with Japan in 1945, because of our heavy military investment and position in the Ryukyus, of which Okinawa is the largest island. The Ryukyus are the chain of islands that extends southward almost to Taiwan. Naha, the capital of Okinawa, is right next to Taiwan. In fact, from Ishigaki, the island in the chain that is farthest to the southwest, you can actually see Taiwan. The agreement that Nixon and Kissinger signed called for a $25 million gift that we said we would give to Japan to help reunite the Ryukyus with the mainland.

The Japanese government decided that the way they would go about this would be by staging a world's fair, primarily involving their principal trading partners, which were heavily in Asia and the Middle East. They decided that the theme for the world's fair would be oceanography and the sea around us. The idea was to focus on international scientific research into the future of the world's deep oceans. As I said then, it was the right subject in the right country at the right time. It was the moment when the world began to realize how important the oceans are to our future. In the past, countries, like the United States, with large landmasses and abundant natural resources had looked at the sea as a place to fish or swim. But dwindling fossil fuels and soaring prices put large nations in the same boat as smaller countries and led to a series of conferences. The most significant of these were the Law of the Sea Conferences sponsored by the United Nations which led to the signing of the Law of the Sea Convention in 1982.

Most of the exhibits at the world's fair focused on remedial steps, ways to reverse pollution and other threats to the oceans, such as the destruction of its vital resources. The deep oceans had been a no-man's-land and consequently everyone's land. The time had come for decisions to be made about how to distribute the resources scientists were discovering in the oceans, especially on the ocean floor. The spirit of the Okinawa exposition was that nations ought to share their technical information about the oceans with each other.

It sounds pretty obscure today, even far-fetched, but in the mid-1970s discussions of the deep seabed inevitably came around to the subject of manganese nodules. These were chunks of ore made primarily of cobalt and manganese, two important minerals that the United States had to import. The countries we imported them from, including Brazil, Australia, and some African nations, had begun to consume most of what they produced. That turned the focus to the oceans, where these manganese nodules covered hundreds of thousands of square miles of the seabed. The United States

FAREWELL, AMBASSADOR LANE

Lane family gathers round the cake.

Five-person geta gang, foot racing idea originally from Japan—now from the pages of Sunset. Or is the family just following in Bill's footsteps?

Ken Hively

Relaxing following Bill's swearing-in ceremony as Ambassador to Expo '75 at the White House are Vice President Nelson Rockefeller, Mrs. Lane, Ambassador Lane and Japanese Ambassador to the U.S., Takeshi Yasukawa.

Montage of images from *Stet*, July 7, 1975, giving Ambassador Lane a festive send-off.

was the leader in developing the technology to extract these and other resources from the seabed, although it was a very expensive process. Things turned out differently, but at the time, we assumed that manganese nodules would become a vital natural resource, one that would be especially important in our Cold War economic competition with the Soviet Union.

I took a strong interest in these matters. I had long been involved with water- and ocean-related issues. I was an early investor in Sea Life Park in Hawaii, and I had been invited to be a part of the Law of the Sea Conference, another opportunity I had to pass up. I was also familiar with the Pacific, in part through my involvement in the Japan-California Association (later the Japan Western Association) and the Pacific Basin Economic Council, and of course PATA, so that I personally knew a lot of the key people in government and business. President Ford and Secretary Kissinger both knew of my interests and of the breadth of my background in the Pacific, and this was why Kissinger asked me to serve as the commissioner general of our exhibit pavilion, with the rank of ambassador.

As part of my preparation, I had a series of briefings in Washington. It turned out that I knew a hell of a lot about the history of world's fairs. I loved the San Francisco World's Fair of 1939 when I was a kid, and my dad was very much involved in the organization of Treasure Island for that event. So I had a lot of literature and knew more about it than any of my briefers in Washington.

Our participation in the world's fair was organized through the United States Information Service, an arm of the State Department. There were forty-five other countries that were invited to participate. We were the lead country, but the Soviet Union, Iran and Iraq, Saudi Arabia and Egypt, Australia and New Zealand, Taiwan and Korea, and other Japanese trading partners also participated. China did not have an exhibit. Of the forty-six countries, many were represented by diplomats holding the rank of ambassador, and all held the title commissioner general. Collectively they formed the College of Exhibitors. This body had to deal with the host government on all kinds of problems, things like housing and utilities (air-conditioning was vitally important on Okinawa), coordinating the visiting dignitaries— just a mess of problems. Rather than have each commissioner general deal with the host government, the congress elected a chairman to coordinate everything. I was named chairman.

It turned out that State Department people assumed that the U.S. ambassador would only visit the world's fair on occasion, usually for ceremonial events like the opening and closing ceremonies and the host country's national day. This had been the case with other world's fairs overseas. In fact, not too many of my fellow commissioners chose to move to Okinawa. But it never entered my head that that was the assumption, so from the minute I said I'd be interested in the assignment and talked it over with Jean, it was always in my mind that this was going to precipitate a move of our family.

I checked into the Department of Defense schools, which our children would be attending on Okinawa, and found that they were very good schools. I went over there beforehand and checked into housing. I found a home that had been started in construction for Admiral Nimitz right after the Battle of Okinawa. The atom bomb subsequently precluded his moving from Guam to Okinawa for the planned invasion of Japan, so he never lived in the house. The house was completed, however, and it was owned by an executive of Foremost Dairy, which had a big contract with the military. I arranged to rent this home for one year. The Motobu Peninsula, where the fair was located, now a beautiful resort area with lovely beaches and hotels, was quite a distance from the house, so I rented a very fine cabin cruiser from a company up in Seattle.

Senator Charles Percy, chairman of the Senate Foreign Relations Committee, did not ask me to resign my positions at *Sunset*, so I could continue as publisher and president, conducting most of my *Sunset* business by telephone and correspondence. I came back to Menlo Park at my own expense on several occasions, and I used the opportunity to visit Washington and report to Secretary Kissinger. And Mel and his wife, Joan, came to Okinawa for a visit.

I put a lot of energy into helping organize the U.S. pavilion. We needed a big, impressive exhibit. Drawing on my connections at Lockheed, in Sunnyvale, I was able to get the company to make a mock-up of a new technology it had developed, where you took warm surface ocean water and cold deep-sea water and produced a working fluid that could be vaporized to turn turbines and generators to produce electricity. They had set up a test model and operated it off of the big island of Hawaii right near the Mauna Kea Beach Hotel. The process was expensive, but at a time when the cost of fossil fuels was soaring, it seemed to be worth the investment. That Lockheed mock-up was our key exhibit. I got a lot of electronic gear from Hewlett-Packard, which helped us in some of our other exhibits. We also got moon rocks, which was a big deal at the time. They were hard to get, but I persuaded NASA to let us have them, and the Japanese went wild over them.

We had a beautiful pavilion. It was just a knockout. It was composed of seven large modules. In one of them, huge overhead models, photos, and videos from four orbiting satellites—ERTS, Skylab, Nimbus, and GEO-SAT—showed the interactions between oceans and the skies that affect weather and ocean currents. In all, the U.S. pavilion contained forty-two separate exhibits, comprising 167 individual displays that told the story of America's involvement with the sea. The pavilion was the result of co-operation between government agencies, private industry, and a host of institutions of education and research, which provided advice, research, and technical materials, including a rich library. As commissioner general, I plowed into this. I took over this beautiful corner office overlooking the ocean from the Motobu Peninsula, which was a very important battlefield in the Battle of Okinawa. A little island that I could see from my office was where Ernie Pyle had been killed.

The College of Exhibitors met at the beginning, and once or twice during the six months, and then at the end for the closing ceremonies in January 1976, when Crown Prince Akihito, now the emperor, closed the exposition. In between I was authorized to speak on behalf of all the participating countries. I met a large number of senior people from corporations, particularly Japanese corporations. Sony, Toyota, and most of the large Japanese companies had big corporate exhibits at that world's fair. We entertained a lot, and they did as well, so I established numerous contacts.

I had traveled to Japan before, and I was very interested in Japanese history and the Japanese culture. Jean was also interested in it, and she got very much involved. Our two youngest children, Bob and Brenda, went to the Department of Defense schools on Okinawa. Sharon, our daughter in college, taught English in a Japanese school. It was a great cultural experience and a wonderful family experience. Culturally, the kids got a lot out of it, although Okinawa is very Americanized, and at that time it was even more so than it is now. We bought most of our goods at the PX stores for military personnel and their dependents, but we made a real effort to get the kids out into some of the native villages, and our housekeeper invited us to her family home.

We learned a lot about Okinawa's unique cultural heritage. One of my security guards took us to his father's funeral, a ceremony that was quite different on Okinawa than it would have been on the mainland of Japan. If you go through the cemeteries on Okinawa, you see Portuguese names, Dutch names, and so on. And there were a lot of intermarriages with the Chinese, with the native people of Taiwan, and with the Koreans, so that the people of the Ryukyus, particularly on Okinawa, have facial features that are very different from those of the rest of the Japanese. The Ryukyu traditions, dances, songs, and handicrafts are distinctive, with some flavor of the Chinese. One reason it was not part of the main fabric of the Japanese political or cultural scene is that it remained open during the two-hundred-plus-year closure of the mainland islands, and that was the reason Commodore Perry sailed into Naha in 1853: Naha was an open port. That was the year before he negotiated with the shoguns to bring his fleet of so-called Black Ships to the closed ports, which opened up Japan.

During World War II, Emperor Hirohito did not put any of Okinawa's historical temples and castles on the Red Cross list that we tried to adhere to for our bombing, particular targets that we would try to avoid. We didn't do any bombing in places like Kyoto or the Imperial Palace because they were on the list, but we just plastered the Ryukyus, Okinawa in particular— although by 1975 it had been rebuilt. Today Okinawa is one of the major tourist destinations, where there are beautiful beach hotels and pineapple plantations. It's just a lovely island, as it was when I lived there in 1975–76.

The International Exposition very definitely helped to reestablish and reunite the Ryukyus with the mainland. We made fantastic inroads in helping to achieve what Kissinger and Nixon had hoped for in 1972. The Ryukyus had always been separate from the mainland in that they didn't get much milk (meaning attention) from the royal family. As they say on an Iowa farm, it was the left-hind tit. It's the left-hind tit that doesn't get much milk for the little piglet that's stuck down there, while the other piglets are getting all the milk before it gets that far. This situation began to change in 1975. Through the personal contacts fostered by the International Exposition, relations between mainland Japan and Okinawa markedly improved.

Down Under

I returned to *Sunset* in the summer of 1976, and from that point on, government service continually beckoned. Not long after my return, I was appointed chairman of the California Desert Conservation Area Advisory Committee. Rogers Morton, interior secretary under Nixon and Ford, appointed me chairman of the original task force, and then I was elected chairman by the members of the advisory committee. In that capacity I facilitated the creation of the landmark legislation governing the California desert.

As a result of my work on national parks, water issues, and the environment, my name was more than once placed in consideration for the position of secretary of the interior. It got most serious in 1970, when Secretary Walter Hickel was fired by President Nixon after Hickel criticized the Vietnam War. Russell Train was Hickel's deputy, and Russ and I went over to talk with Nixon, and I recall that Anne Armstrong was there. I decided to steer clear of it then, as I did later, during the first Reagan administration, in the early 1980s. At that time, Senator Clifford Hansen, who was very close to Reagan and had been a member of my Centennial Commission on National Parks, wanted to put my name forward. Senator Hansen himself had been asked by Reagan to be interior secretary, but he turned it down. When he did, as he told me later, he said to Reagan, "You've got a fellow Californian who would be ideal, someone I imagine you know."

In fact, I had been chairman of Governor Reagan's environmental confer-ence water section in the early 1970s. Senator Hansen reminded Reagan of my involvement with the U.S. Bureau of Land Management, the desert, the parks, Native Americans, and so on. And interior secretaries tradition-ally come from the West.

So I was asked to come back to Washington, and I met with the presi-dent and William Casey, who had been campaign manager and headed up Reagan's transition team, and some others. They put the question to me directly: "If we were to put your name forward, would you consider accept-ing?" They didn't want to get a name out there and then have the person say no and create a lot of embarrassment. For a number of reasons, in that first Reagan term I said that I did not want a full-time appointment, but that I would welcome an opportunity to serve on a commission of some sort. I later learned from Edwin Meese, Reagan's attorney general, that if I had agreed to put my name in the hat, the president was prepared to ap-point me. Instead I was appointed to the National Productivity Advisory Committee, chaired by William Simon.

Turning aside the secretary of the interior position was not especially difficult for me, because it's just a bone-crushing job. You have to have a pretty hard hide to withstand all the pressures, especially those concern-ing the Bureau of Land Management, which is involved in a lot of mining and a lot of leasing of lands, including leasing for offshore oil drilling and other projects that make money for the federal government. It's not widely known, because it doesn't get nearly the same amount of attention, but running the Department of Interior is almost as complicated as running the Pentagon, where the various military services—Army, Navy, Marine Corps, Air Force—have to cooperate in order to get together to build, say, a single type of helicopter, with modifications to suit the particular needs of each branch of service. Interior was the same way. At times it seems almost impossible, a Pandora's box. I got a sense of this from working with two or three Interior secretaries, so I didn't particularly want to leap into that job. Also, I didn't want to give up *Sunset* at that time, as I would have had to do. But I did indicate that maybe by the second term I would be interested in a full-time appointment.

Well, about halfway into the first Reagan term, Secretary of the Interior James Watt had become a very controversial and unpopular figure. Again I was asked if I would be interested in being considered for the job and again I declined. I did consider the idea for the second Reagan term. I talked to Jean about it, and to Mel about an extended absence from *Sunset*. But I just didn't see how I could do what needed to be done in that short period of time—three or three and a half years after my Senate confirmation. And although I knew Vice President Bush very well and might have been reappointed by him, I decided I just didn't want to take it on.

I was glad I made that decision, because shortly after Reagan was elected to a second term in 1984, I was asked to become the U.S. ambassador to Australia. Here was an opportunity I could not pass up. I had my hands full with *Sunset* and I didn't particularly want to leave the country, but the kids had by now grown up and I was especially attracted to the assignment. I knew Australia very well. In fact, I had briefed Governor and Mrs. Reagan before they visited Australia in the early 1970s, when they represented President Nixon on a tour around the Pacific. So President Reagan was well aware of my background, as was Secretary of Defense Caspar Weinberger, which was important because the Australia assignment had a lot to do

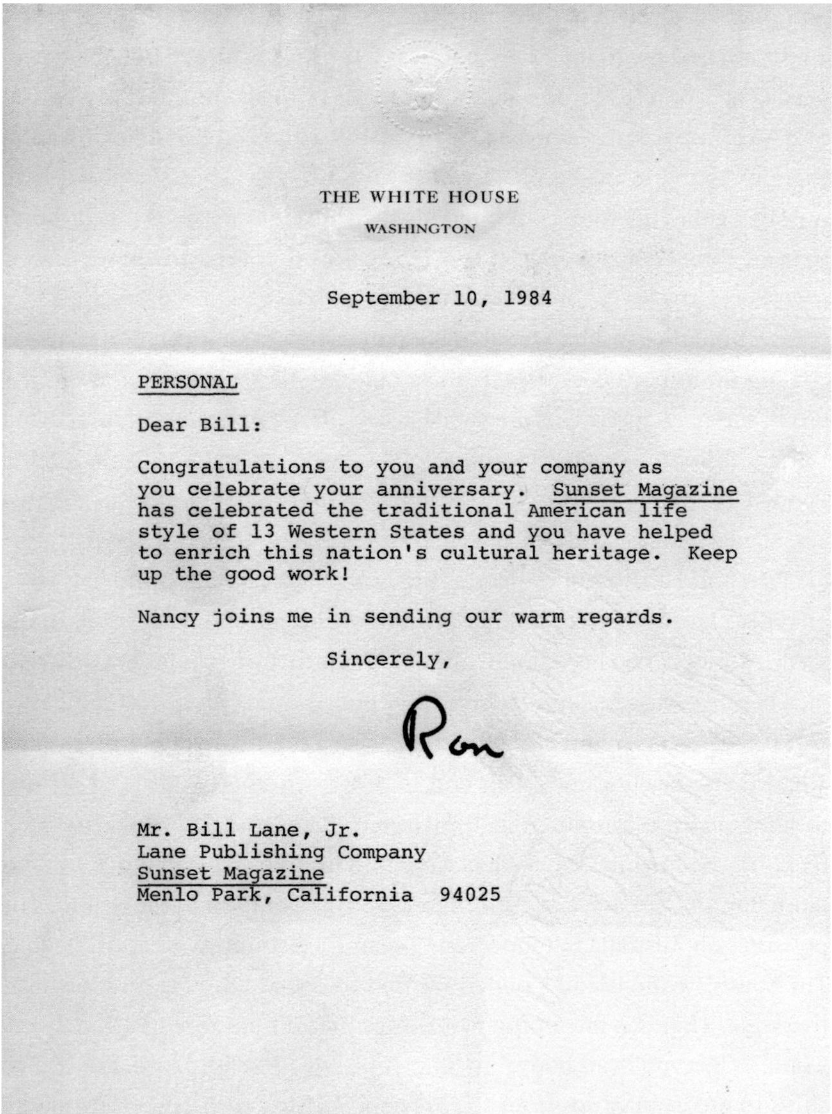

THE WHITE HOUSE
WASHINGTON

September 10, 1984

PERSONAL

Dear Bill:

Congratulations to you and your company as you celebrate your anniversary. Sunset Magazine has celebrated the traditional American life style of 13 Western States and you have helped to enrich this nation's cultural heritage. Keep up the good work!

Nancy joins me in sending our warm regards.

Sincerely,

Ron

Mr. Bill Lane, Jr.
Lane Publishing Company
Sunset Magazine
Menlo Park, California 94025

President Ronald Reagan writes to congratulate Bill Lane on the occasion of the 55th anniversary of Lane publication of *Sunset*.

135

with military security vis-à-vis the Soviet Union. Also, I knew CIA chief Bill Casey very well, and Casey's opinion counted for a lot, because the KGB operations for all of Southeast Asia were headquartered in Australia.

I used to read *Foreign Affairs* magazine, where there was a lot of complaining about political appointees buying their way into ambassadorships. Not a few people, I'm sure, assumed that this was the case with my own appointment. The fact is, I don't think I ever gave more than $5,000 or $10,000 to Reagan's election campaigns, and I definitely was not involved in the campaign. Even had I wanted to do more, I couldn't afford it in those days. I mean, a $100,000 gift? I just didn't have that kind of money to spend in my *Sunset* days.

Once I agreed to take the job, I remember sitting down with Secretary of State George Shultz to talk about the job, before the vote on my appointment took place in the Senate Foreign Relations Committee. Secretary Shultz advised me to mend my political fences. As it turned out, no fences needed mending, as I won a unanimous vote of the committee. My official title was United States ambassador to Australia and the Republic of Nauru, that tiny island in the Pacific Ocean.

Then came the rounds of briefings in Washington. The fact is, I didn't have any briefers at State, Defense, CIA, or any other department who knew more about the Pacific or Australia than I did. I didn't know every aspect, of course; in particular I had to be briefed on some of the legislation that was coming up in both countries. For example, we had a big aviation donnybrook with the Australians on airline access after Pan American folded and United Airlines was vying for increased access in Australia. As ambassador, I ended up spending a good deal of my time on this issue, and I negotiated and signed a major aviation agreement.

Jean and I arrived in Canberra, the Australian capital, in the first week of 1986. Right away, I found that most of my attention was devoted to the security issues I had been boning up on. The situation was potentially serious, because New Zealand had recently pulled out of the ANZUS alliance (ANZUS being an acronym for Australia–New Zealand–United States). That alliance effectively came to an end in 1984, when New Zealand refused to allow nuclear vessels from the United States and elsewhere to enter its ports. Meanwhile, the Soviets were building up their presence in Cam Ranh Bay, in Vietnam, and running a big KGB operation in the region. The pressures on Australia to follow New Zealand's example were considerable. The South Pacific Island Council wanted to declare the region a nuclear-free zone. That was one of the first things that hit me when I arrived, and I said, "Over my dead body." At that time, we were using nuclear-armed ships to escort oil ships from the Persian Gulf to Japan and elsewhere in the Far East, so the last thing we wanted to get involved with was nuclear-free zones.

Reagan and his advisors were very concerned, because if we lost Australia, we would lose the joint facilities that monitored Soviet nuclear testing. At that time the United States was conducting most of its monitoring by means of three satellites: one over the United Kingdom, one over the United States, and one over the Philippines. What we said was that we used these satellites to monitor the nuclear testing of the Soviet Union—but in fact we were monitoring India and China too, primarily from the downlink station at Pine Gap, which is right outside Alice Springs in Australia. There were two other joint facilities: one a low-frequency-radio below-surface submarine communication

center for all the allies' submarines in the Pacific and in the Indian Ocean, and another for the air force in Woomera, in South Australia.

This was all classified information at the time. The Australians were not aware that we were also monitoring China and India for nuclear testing. The Australians were very sensitive about that, because they had trade and other relationships with those two countries, and they didn't want to be perceived as spying on them. So Australia was a very key part of the world, our only ally in the South Pacific after New Zealand pulled out. This huge island continent is about the size of the continental United States, with a small population equivalent to that of Southern California spread across it.

Later on, I would hear people say things like, well, this was the era of Mikhail Gorbachev and arms control treaties and the winding down of the Cold War. But the fact is, nobody saw the end of the tunnel in the Cold War in 1985. My chief accomplishment as ambassador was helping to maintain the integrity of the bilateral defense treaties between the United States and Australia and to renew the agreements for the crucial joint facilities that made possible our surveillance and intelligence operations.

Bill and Jean Lane with Governor General Sir Ninian Stephen, at Admiralty House, Sydney, January 7, 1986, on the occasion of the presentation to His Excellency the Governor-General of Letters of Credence by L. W. Lane, Ambassador-Designate of the United States of America.

Trade was another sensitive issue during my Australia assignment. We had a lot of problems with Australia on subsidized grain and rice and sugar, because we were very competitive with them in the Pacific. Trade matters spilled over into security, because Australia was a trading partner with the Soviet Union, selling wheat in particular. Yet Australia couldn't make a secret of the fact that it was part of the Western alliance in the Cold War.

These were delicate issues that the American ambassador had to stay on top of. I thought it would make good sense for the Australian prime minister to make his country's case directly to the U.S. Congress. So I proposed the idea to House Speaker Jim Wright, who recommended it to the White House. President Reagan endorsed the proposal that the Australian prime minister be invited to address a joint session of Congress, a first for an Australian leader. It was just at that moment, on the eve of the Australian prime minister's visit to Washington, in June 1988, that the Department of Agriculture decided to authorize a sale of subsidized grain to Indonesia. They said it was crucial to the U.S. economy, and maybe they thought it was, but from my perspective we needed this Indonesia deal like a hole in the head. I flew back to Washington and met with James Baker, who was then secretary of the treasury, and I told him that I strenuously objected to the idea. I knew he was close to Reagan because he had recently served as his chief of staff. Baker saw my point, and he took the matter to Vice President Bush and persuaded him to stop the sale.

One of the great challenges of running an embassy is coordinating all the different departments. In Canberra I had thirteen agencies to coordinate. Defense was good. Agriculture was good. The FBI is under Justice, and Justice was good. Commerce was very important and very good. The CIA was very good. The State Department, in my experience, was the most difficult to manage. State always felt competitive, much more so than was necessary, in my opinion, and was often at odds with Commerce, Agriculture, and Defense. A big part of my job was to keep all those wires from getting tangled.

The State Department would like everyone to think, as most people actually do, that the foreign embassy is "the State Department," when in fact it's frequently a minority in terms of the numbers of personnel. In my embassy, Defense alone was twice the size of the State Department staff, because you had the Army, the Navy, and the Marine Corps, all of which reported to me, not just for Australia but for the whole South Pacific. I had six pilots on my staff, for my official plane, who rotated as pilots and had desk jobs.

In its briefings, the State Department wanted to give the impression that the ambassador couldn't do anything without working through the secretary of state, but in the real world the constitutional authority is the letter of authority from the president: the ambassador ultimately reports to the president of the United States. The State Department would like you never to contact, say, the secretary of defense directly, but rather to go through the secretary of state. But I told Secretary Shultz at the very beginning, "I certainly will keep you informed on the security issues, but I'm going to work directly with Secretary Weinberger, too."

One clash in particular I had with the State Department stands out in my memory. I wanted to get an emissary of the president to come down to represent our country on the anniversary of the Battle of the Coral Sea. I had asked for a cabinet officer, and Secretary Baker was supposed to come down but had to cancel at the last minute. The word came back that the State Department did not want a replacement, that it was just a ceremonial event so no special arrangements were necessary. In fact, it was a very significant event for the Australian government and people, but the matter was being decided by some desk person back in Washington who probably didn't

To Bill Lane – With appreciation, every good wish & Warm Regard
Ronald Reagan

President Ronald Reagan and Ambassador Lane, circa 1985.

know a damn thing about World War II. For the Australians, the Battle of the Coral Sea, in May 1942, was what had saved them from the Japanese invasion. The annual anniversary is very important, and a representative from the president had been coming down for thirty years.

"Well, we can't get anybody down there," I was informed. This was about thirty-six hours before the event, and I knew that the only way I could make it happen would be to get a dedicated plane from the Department of Defense or the White House. So I went directly to the president, and he called Cap Weinberger, and we got the secretary of the army and his wife on a Defense Department airplane. They came out in about twenty-four hours. The State Department types were madder than hell that I had gone over their heads. I made what I thought was the correct decision. It had nothing to do with personality clashes or egos.

I'm always trying to override the personality conflicts and bring out the best in people in order to make things work. An example was right there in the embassy in Canberra, where I brought in more junior officers to our weekly staff meetings, called country officer meetings. My deputy chief of mission recommended that we have only heads of departments at our meetings, but I said I wanted to enlist assistant heads of departments. Their inclusion made a very nice impression on these younger people and enriched our weekly discussions.

Years earlier, the State Department had made the case, and there was some validity to it, that the Department of Commerce representative, the commercial officer, should be located in Sydney and not in Canberra, because Sydney is where most of the business is conducted. At the same time, they had excluded that officer from the country officer meeting because of what they said was the inconvenience and the cost of transportation. I immediately said, "To hell with that." Canberra to Sydney is like San Francisco to Los Angeles. The way I looked at it, one good trade deal would pay for the officer's trip to and from Canberra a thousand times over.

The job of ambassador involves a lot of entertaining, and Jean and I had our hands full at the residence, which was a whirlwind of activity, with events planned for almost every day of the week. There were countless official receptions at the ambassador's residence, a classic Colonial Williamsburg home, which was built during World War II. In 1943, as Allied forces battled the Japanese in New Guinea, First Lady Eleanor Roosevelt visited the residence, which was still under construction. It is said that her tour of the site went along smoothly until she saw the library fireplace and, memorably, pronounced the opening too small to draw properly. Despite her objections, the original design remained intact, and in fact we found that the fireplace drew perfectly.

Jean oversaw the redesign of the interior of the official residence, which proved to be a big job. The furnishings, especially the textiles and general decor, had not kept a uniform Colonial feel through the years of revolving occupants. Jean knows more than a thing or two about interior design, so she took charge of redecorating the residence. Standing on a grassy knoll studded with majestic eucalyptus trees, the residence overlooks several garden areas, and Jean took full advantage by applying her gardening expertise. No matter what the month, she could always find something in bloom to create flower arrangements. Jean brought a touch of *Sunset* to the grounds of the residence by cultivating an undeveloped area along the back driveway as a vegetable garden, planting tomatoes, zucchini, green beans, and corn, as well as salad greens like radicchio and French sorrel.

We celebrated each Fourth of July with a festive barbecue at the residence, and the Australian holidays also punctuated our calendar. In March 1989, I donned Western attire, including a ten-gallon hat and spurs, to ride a quarter horse as marshal in the grand parade at the Royal Easter Show in

Sydney. An emotional highlight of our tour was the January 26, 1988, celebration of Australia Day, marking the two-hundredth anniversary of the settlement of Australia.

My assignment as ambassador ended in mid-April 1989, but I stayed on, at President Bush's request, to escort Vice President Dan Quayle on his tour of Australia. I declined President Bush's invitation to continue in the Australian post. It was time to get back to *Sunset*—although not for long, as it turned out.

Selling *Sunset*

My experiences in Australia gave me an even stronger appreciation of the role Western America played in the U.S. economy and the growing influence it had in the Pacific Basin. I was eager to apply that knowledge to the publication of *Sunset* magazine. In my absence, Mel served as board chairman of Lane Publishing Company and publisher of *Sunset* magazine and books. We were in constant touch, and I came back here several times. I was allowed to remain on the board, because it was a family-held business, but I couldn't receive any compensation. Upon my return, in May 1989, Mel and I served as co-chairmen of Lane Publishing, and I once again took up my position as publisher of *Sunset* magazine, while Mel continued as publisher of *Sunset* Books.

Mel and Bill Lane at the entrance to *Sunset* after Bill's return from Australia.

I immediately went out into the field and met with readers and met every governor in the thirteen Western states to learn the market, the changes that had taken place in my absence. Mel, meanwhile, had begun to make the case for the sale of *Sunset*, but I was raring to go and so my first reaction was to wave off the idea. I remember telling him, "No way do I want to sell." Don Logan of Time Inc. had come out to Australia to talk about selling the magazine, but I said to him I wouldn't even consider it. I planned to go back to *Sunset* and go back full bore.

Mel and I had talked about what should happen in case one of us got hit by a truck—or both of us, because we sometimes traveled together. We wanted our widows and our heirs to know how we felt about certain things. The Lanes were the sole owners of *Sunset*. Mel and I had bought our first stock after we moved to Menlo Park, in the early 1950s. I remember going to American Trust and borrowing $15,000—it felt like $15 million!—in order to buy our first stock. Just the family owned stock. Mel and I owned 60 percent, and the children owned 40 percent. I had three children and Mel had two, so in order to even things out, our mother, Ruth Bell Lane, had given some of her stock to Mel so that the families had equal stock.

Over the years, we never considered mergers. We didn't want debt, we didn't want finance capital, and we didn't want to lose any of our ownership. We were very healthy and growing and making a profit. We weren't trying to be the world's biggest, and we had no stockholders to answer to. We were happy and working hard and doing very well. So debt, financing, going public to get more money, merging, some of the opportunities that might have been there—we didn't even spend any time looking. The hardcore *Sunset* books—the garden book, the barbecue book, the best cookbook, salads, and so on—based mostly on research and writing from the magazine, brought in 90 percent of the business, and a little bit more than 90 percent of the profit because we could have such long runs and reprints on those books. So in any merger we would never have gotten credit for the franchise we have on the goose laying the golden egg, which was the editorial content of the magazine.

In any case, Mel eventually persuaded me that it was time to sell. I saw that we were a little further along than my dad was, at age fifty-five, when he brought in Howard Willoughby as general manager with the understanding that Howard would mentor us in the management of the business. There was also the changing landscape of the communications industry in the 1980s, which favored larger and larger media companies. We concluded that the long-range health and future growth of *Sunset* and career opportunities for its staff would be best accomplished by a merger with a quality national publishing firm.

Surprise! We couldn't let this birthday slip by, Bill

Bill Lane in a photo montage that appeared in *Stet* on the occasion of his seventieth birthday, in November 1989.

Sunset had come to be considered the real plum of the whole industry. Time Inc. had been coming to my father for many years, and most of the big companies, such as Hearst, Condé Nast, and Newhouse, had expressed interest. Sam Newhouse flew out from New York, and Mel and I had breakfast with him. When we decided that we would consider selling, we went through the list of people who had called on us, and one or two others. Rupert Murdoch had been around for a long time. In Australia, when he came out from New York, Jean and I were guests at his home several times, and he had several of his people call on us in California over the years. There was also Robert Maxwell and Densu in Japan, but I made a ground rule right at the beginning—and Mel agreed—that we would consider no foreign ownership. This included Murdoch, even though he was an American citizen and News Corporation, his parent company, was incorporated in the United States.

We went through about ten different companies, and we selected six—Reader's Digest, Time Warner, Hearst, Condé Nast, Newhouse, and Meredith—which signed the agreement that pledged them to maintain the confidentiality of the complete breakdown of all Lane Publishing finances, which were all private in our company and which we didn't want to reveal. We didn't even want to make known the fact that we were interested in selling, so this all had to be done in secrecy. It was done only with the CEOs and the CFOs of each company, each of whom had to sign a statement of confidentiality.

Sunset's selling price couldn't be based on its earnings, because we never put a priority on earnings. We made a good profit, and we shared the profit with the employees, providing good benefits, but the stockholders never maximized. In fact, we tried to keep as much cash in the company as possible, up to the limit that our attorneys said the IRS would allow. *Sunset* continued to be run like a family business, continued to refuse ads for several categories of products, including liquor and cigarettes. The magazine's circulation in 1990 was roughly 1.4 million. The median age of *Sunset* readers, we estimated, was thirty-seven, and about half were male.

We had a minimum figure for our assets. We owned all of our real estate, including our headquarters buildings, and we owned a big ranch, five thousand acres of prime land up in Northern California, plus eighteen beautiful residential acres in Menlo Park. That was all Lane Publishing. We had a lot of cash, and we had a franchise. There was no one who could even touch us when it came to Western America, and certain companies had a lot to gain by getting the *Sunset* identification and the access, not just to publishing *Sunset* but to our friends, to our readership for promotion, if they had other magazines.

On March 27, 1990, we announced an agreement in principle for the sale of *Sunset* to Time Warner. The deal was signed on June 1. Time Warner paid the Lanes $225 million: $80 million in cash and $145 million in preferred stock. Mel and I signed a five-year non-compete agreement with Time Warner, during which period we served as consultants. Time Warner didn't want the ranch or the residential real estate, so these were deducted from the sales price at appraised value. Mel and I subsequently sold those properties.

Selling *Sunset* produced a tectonic shift in my life, you could say. I had been part of the company officially for almost forty-five years, although my involvement in our family business extended back to my boyhood, when Dad bought the magazine in 1928 and moved our family out to California. At the time of the sale, I was only seventy years old. As I looked back on it two decades later, I knew that Mel and I had made the right move. I've been able to do a lot of exciting things since then—although I could never find time to do them all.

Bill and Jean at Half Dome in 2000.

Chapter 6

A Man in Motion

Citizen Lane

At sunset on November 15, 1872, the five-wick lard oil lamp inside the Fresnel lens of the Pigeon Point Lighthouse was lit for the first time. Pigeon Point, perched on a cliff along the central California coast, about fifty miles south of San Francisco, is one of the tallest lighthouses in the United States. The lens, made of 1,008 prisms, stands sixteen feet tall, is six feet in diameter, and weighs 8,000 pounds. The lantern room that houses it was constructed at the United States Lighthouse Service's general depot in New York and then shipped around the Horn. The original Fresnel lens cast a light visible up to twenty miles away. It no longer functions, but the lighthouse, today using a twenty-four-inch Aero Beacon, still serves as an active U.S. Coast Guard aid to navigation.

I visited Pigeon Point as a boy, when my family lived in Burlingame. In the 1930s, I viewed it while at sea aboard a commercial vessel, and then twice more while passing by on a navy ship during World War II. Pigeon Point acquired special significance for the entire Lane family in November 2005, when the Peninsula Open Space Trust (POST) celebrated the opening of the "Mel's Lane" trail at Pigeon Point Light Station State Historic Park, along Highway 1 near Pescadero. Mel's Lane is part of the California Coastal Trail. The quarter-mile trail segment in his name is meant to honor his work as the first chairman of the California Coastal Commission and a founder of POST.

All these factors, as well as my enthusiasm for the history of the West, inspired me to become a major donor behind a $6 million campaign, still under way, to restore and reopen Pigeon Point Lighthouse after a section of the cornice on the exterior of the lighthouse fell off in December 2001 and the structure was closed to the public.

The sale of *Sunset* in 1990 opened up all kinds of possibilities for me (as well as for Mel) to become active in the field of philanthropy. Not long after the sale of the Lane Publishing Company, Mel and I surprised many of our friends—and even some of our family—by moving together to 3000 Sand Hill Road in adjoining offices—supported there by a small but loyal staff. We had earlier taken an option to buy the land to relocate *Sunset* and later turned it over to architect Thomas Ford, our good friend and the driving force in making Sand Hill Road an epicenter of venture capital and, like Mel and me, a co-founder of POST. Ford creatively adapted a residential style of architecture and landscaping that made 3000 Sand Hill Road a world-famous suburban office complex.

Using that office as my base of operations, I began giving a lot more time and charitable contributions to a number of causes. I had begun to champion many of these same causes as publisher of *Sunset*. In fact, my gift giving went as far back as 1946, when I received $500 severance pay after getting off the navy troopship. I gave $250 of that total to the Salvation Army, because that organization had helped me to put in a library when our ship was in port, before we went back out to sea with another load of troops. The remaining $250 I gave to Stanford University, my alma mater.

My numerous and quite varied adventures in philanthropy after Mel and I sold *Sunset* kept me nearly as busy as I'd ever been. My wife, Jean, has a point when she says that I don't know the meaning of the word "retire." I have kept in touch with my Time Warner successors at *Sunset* and, as emeritus publisher, have even been invited to collaborate with them on a project or two. One thing I miss from my publishing days is the staff. At *Sunset* I could enlist various people to work on a new project, but I no longer have that luxury. Karen Hamilton, my assistant for nearly thirty years, has proved invaluable to me, but there were a lot of projects we couldn't take on by ourselves.

There is no Lane Foundation, just something we call the Bill and Jean Lane Fund, whose base of operations is our dining room table in our Portola Valley home. Jean and I have been major donors to some very significant causes, as well as to many smaller, equally important ones. A special focus of our philanthropy has been the environment, parks, conservation, open space, and historic preservation. A lot of the money in our lifetime—and a lot of it after we're gone—will be used to support worthy endeavors.

I have long tried to be a solid citizen of my local community. I'm reminded of this priority to "think local" by something my friend George Shultz once said, words to the effect that, "Before we try to save the world, we should care for our own neighborhood." Jean and I have been big boosters of local volunteerism. In fact, it was *Sunset* that first got me interested in volunteerism. As we researched *Sunset* articles on, for example, saving an old building, we found that it often took a lot of volunteerism to take an old house off the tax rolls, to zone it non-commercial, or whatever was involved in the effort to preserve it. Local businesses might have an interest, local individuals might have an interest, but usually there needed to be a lot of grassroots volunteerism in order to win city council or board of supervisors approval for one measure or another.

Certainly *Sunset* led to my getting involved in my community of Portola Valley after we moved up here in the 1950s. Today the town is mainly rural, with a population of less than five thousand—although it might have turned out quite differently. Half a century ago, folks who lived out here in what was once unincorporated San Mateo County got a wake-up call, right after Jean and I moved to the valley, when we heard about a proposal for a motel and restaurant where our beloved Ford Field is now located. For me and others it was an early "call to arms." We knew our beautiful Western hills were at risk of being overdeveloped, and we rallied together to incorporate in order to have local government create our own ordinances that would preserve a rural and conservation-oriented way of life. I helped organize the town in 1964, was elected the first mayor, and remained involved in the town's governance.

Jump ahead to 2003. That year, earthquake issues and lack of insurance forced the abandonment of the old Town Center buildings—library, community hall, and town hall—that had been built on the San Andreas Fault more than thirty years earlier as a "temporary" headquarters. Jean and I stepped forward to help lead the effort to get a new Town Center built. We felt a sense of necessity, even a sense of urgency about this. The growth of natural vegetation, especially in wet years, and die-off in dry years, within and completely surrounding Portola Valley heightens the danger from extensive planting of fir and eucalyptus trees for landscaping and windbreaks and from hundreds of acres of wild pasture grass, often along roads and surrounding homes. This poses a serious threat for a local replay of the catastrophic 1992 Oakland fire that destroyed nearly three thousand single-family homes, killed 25 people, and injured 150 others.

Add to this fire hazard the *inevitability* of a major earthquake, which could cause a broken gas main or topple a residential gas water heater, and you begin to see that a town hall is an absolute priority as a headquarters for volunteers, staff, and consultants to gather and to govern in a time of emergency with maximum safety and to operate a state-of-the-art emergency-preparedness center. Jean and I made the lead gift (pledged "anonymously" immediately following the unanimous approval by the town council for the new Town Center) and got the ball rolling. Eventually, private donations covered roughly 80 percent of the total cost of the project.

The site chosen was the original location of the Portola Valley Schoolhouse. The result, completed in October 2008, is a beautiful complex of three green structures on a remarkable thirteen-acre campus of fields and playgrounds. We now look back and ask, "Why didn't we do it sooner?"

I take great pride not only in the finished product but in the way it was undertaken and accomplished, which involved a process of environmentally conscious planning and construction, with lots of community input and involvement. In the spirit of the town's charter, which embraces stewardship of open space as one of its founding principles, public workshops were held to establish requirements for the new facilities. The town council and the residents who participated in the workshops were determined to adhere to exceptionally high environmental standards. The town established goals to increase natural landscape, reduce site coverage, and restore a stream that had been buried in a culvert when the old schoolhouse was built. These green aspects proved decisive in attracting private funding support for the project.

As the seismically unsafe old Town Center was dismantled, materials from the buildings were incorporated into the new structures as beams, paneling, countertops, and structural fill—in fact, about a quarter of all wood used was reclaimed wood. As a result of these and other measures, construction carbon emissions were reduced by 32 percent. Buildings were kept modestly sized and built low, so as not to obstruct the views. And a premium was put on native landscape and pasture grass.

The new Town Center combines oak woodlands, playing fields, and new buildings (a library, a town hall, and an emergency-operations center) to create a civic center that lives up to the town's goal of achieving maximum harmony with the natural beauty of the landscape and the environment. I took special satisfaction when this project was singled out for excellence by the American Institute of Architects (AIA), *Sunset* magazine's longtime partner in sponsoring an awards competition for architectural design. The AIA's Committee on the Environment chose the new Portola Valley Town Center as a Top Ten Green Project for 2009.

Stanford Ties

I maintain connections to several academic institutions, and since retiring from *Sunset* I have received several honorary degrees, including an honorary L.L.D. from Pomona and (together with Jean) an honorary doctorate from Cal Poly. But it is my ties to Stanford University that are by far the longest and the strongest. In a way, my Stanford connection extends back to the earliest days of *Sunset* magazine.

You have to go back to before the beginning of *Sunset* in 1898. The Southern Pacific fortune, the same wealth that founded *Sunset* magazine, was the reservoir of wealth that founded Stanford University. As one of the Big Four railroad magnates—along with Charles Crocker, Mark Hopkins, and Collis P. Huntington—Leland Stanford co-founded, on June 28, 1861, the Central Pacific Railroad, and was elected its first president. Later that same year, he was elected governor of California, and the railroad's first locomotive was named "Gov. Stanford" in his honor. As head of the Central Pacific, Stanford, wielding a silver hammer, tapped in the famous golden spike in Promontory, Utah, on May 10, 1869, to mark the building of the first transcontinental railway line over the Sierra Nevada. (Governor Stanford kept that spike, and it now resides in the Cantor Museum of Art at Stanford University.) A year earlier, Stanford and his associates had acquired control of the Southern Pacific Railroad, and Stanford was elected its first president, a position he held with only a brief interruption until 1890. In the meantime, in 1885, he founded Stanford University.

It was Stanford University, with its entrepreneurial drive, its pioneering and adventuresome spirit, and the family values behind it, that laid the basis for *Sunset* in the Progressive Era, as historian Kevin Starr so well describes:

> Here was a university which admitted men and women on the same basis and where a significant percentage of students were on scholarship. Here was a university which from the start excelled in such Far Western subjects as mining engineering, geology, economics, and the emergent science of business management. Here was a university whose founding president, David Starr Jordan, a physician by training and an ichthyologist by practice, preached his own version of the strenuous life, based on values of physical fitness, outdoor activity, conservation, a gracious but restrained lifestyle, internationalism, and public service: a pre-figurement, it might be said, of the emergent *Sunset* ethos.

These Stanford-*Sunset* connections became even more explicit after a group of *Sunset* employees led by Charles K. Field bought the magazine from Southern Pacific in 1914. The new owners were strongly loyal to Stanford—and not surprisingly: Field had been a member of Stanford's Pioneer Class, the graduating class of 1895, among whose outstanding figures was an enormously successful mining engineer by the name of Herbert Hoover. Stanford writers made frequent appearances in the magazine, including founding president Jordan and Hoover, whom Starr calls "dual embodiments of the Stanford spirit and the Stanford man in the founding generation." The first issue of Lane *Sunset*, in February 1929, published the text of presidential campaign talks on the importance of family and home given by (Iowa-born!) Hoover, who was then president-elect.

Sunset's Stanford orientation would continue through the two genera-
tions of Lane management and beyond. Over the years, Stanford has issued three publications about *Sunset*: the first was a casebound cookbook
in the 1930s that my mother helped edit as a graduate home economist;
the second, a report on a reader-research project by the Graduate School
of Business in 1938; and in 1998, on the centennial of *Sunset*, the Stanford
Library published a comprehensive bibliography, generously illustrated, of
Sunset's contents in its first hundred years, with introductory historical es-
says, including a magisterial contribution from Kevin Starr, who served for
a decade as California State Librarian. Starr's elaboration on the Stanford-
Sunset commonalities is worth quoting:

> Like Stanford, *Sunset* cherished values of education, conservation, social
> responsibility, and a slightly understated yet enthusiastic lifestyle. Aes-
> thetically, more specifically in terms of architecture and design, *Sunset*,
> like the Stanford campus before it, favored a certain dryness of style in
> dialogue with the water-scarce, semi-arid realities of the Far West. Like
> Stanford University, destined to nurture twentieth-century engineering
> sciences and to generate the computer revolution, *Sunset* had a continu-
> ing belief in practical technology, whose fundamental assumption was:
> The simpler way of doing things was frequently the better way.

The Lane connections to Stanford remain strong down to the present.
Jean and I have made numerous gifts to the university's various programs
and departments, including the Cantor Art Center and Stanford Lively
Arts, and we founded and continued to support the Jean and Bill Lane
Lecture Series. I was a major donor behind the renovation, after the Loma
Prieta earthquake of 1989, of what is now called the Lane History Corner,
dedicated to my mother and father. I have served on the board of overseers
of the Hoover Institution on War, Revolution and Peace. These and other
endeavors have been complemented by Mel's service on Stanford's board
of trustees and his leadership in restoring Memorial Church after the 1989
earthquake.

My Stanford connection extends beyond the campus, to Sacramento,
California's state capital, where I helped lead the effort to rehabilitate and
renovate Governor Stanford's mansion, an effort that got under way in
1991. My approach to fund-raising was influenced by an idea former Stanford president Wallace Sterling gave me early on. He said that you should
have one-third of your fund-raising goal met before you really start to go
out and promote it. That one-third should come as much as possible from
a board of directors, or board of trustees, to reflect their commitment. And
if you don't get that amount from that core group, then you go elsewhere

THE WHITE HOUSE

WASHINGTON

September 16, 1997

L.W. "Bill" Lane, Jr.
3000 Sand Hill Road
Building Two, Suite 215
Menlo Park, California 94025-7113

Dear Bill:

Thanks for your good letter and for the
materials you sent on Stanford. I appreciate
the time you took to put together such an
interesting packet of information and will look
forward to reading it.

Congratulations on the upcoming Centennial of
SUNSET magazine! What a milestone -- you have
real cause to be proud of your involvement and
leadership.

Again, thank you for thinking of us. Hillary
and Chelsea join me in sending you our best
wishes.

Sincerely,

Bill Clinton

in order to get up to about a third before you really start your campaign. That's about how it happened with the Stanford Mansion in Sacramento: first we got one-third in the till, then we launched a public campaign to raise the rest of the money. After I agreed to become "lead dog" (as I like to say) of this effort, I inspired Governor George Deukmejian, Stanford president Donald Kennedy, and local representatives to get on board in a serious way.

In order to achieve success in this kind of fund-raising campaign, you have to be able to articulate a credible rationale for your project—and here, too, I was able to contribute, thanks to my experience as a United States ambassador. I made the case that in a highly competitive economic environment, California, at the time the seventh-largest economy in the world, was poorly equipped to compete in terms of providing an appropriately prestigious setting for hosting those all-important welcoming receptions and business deliberations. We had no official place to receive global, national, and state business and government leaders. In fact, our state was the only one of the top ten states that had no formal reception center in its capital designated for that purpose.

The emperor of Japan and the presidents of Mexico, South Korea, and Greece, not to mention scores of ambassadors, business leaders, and trade representatives, had in recent years come to California and met with the governor and other local representatives. But the hosts often had to use uninspiring state offices, local clubs, and restaurants in the capital to host those important gatherings. That was far from an effective or acceptable way to meet the state's responsibilities. The time had come to have a suitable location in Sacramento where the governor and other state leaders could host important business receptions and negotiations affecting our domestic and foreign trade.

The most promising location was the Leland Stanford Mansion at Eighth and N Streets, just two blocks from the Capitol Building. Built in 1856, and designated a State Historic Park and a National Historic Landmark, the mansion, once California's most important address, offered an ideal setting. Statesmen, foreign envoys, and even presidents had once met there with Governor Stanford and his successors Frederick Low and Henry Haight, until the completion of the Capitol Building in 1869. Countless legislative agreements, business negotiations, and other notable events took place in the mansion during that time, including the completion of the first transcontinental railroad, the acceptance of management for the Yosemite Valley and the Mariposa Grove of Giant Sequoias, laws to protect Asian workers and former slaves, and the creation of the University of California and the California State University systems. This historic building, properly restored, was just what the state government needed.

The renovation of the Leland Stanford Mansion, which in the end cost $22 million, was completed in 2005. It gave me great pleasure to know that the Stanford Mansion, even as it served as a fully functional state office building, continued to open its doors to visitors as a State Historic Park.

Western Horseman

The Leland Stanford Mansion was the birthplace of Leland Junior, the only son of Leland and Jane Lathrop Stanford and the namesake of Stanford University. After Leland Junior died of typhoid in 1884, at age fifteen, while traveling in Italy, his parents founded the university in his memory, and it opened in 1891.

Leland Stanford had begun to purchase the land that would become the university campus starting in 1876, when he acquired Mayfield Grange, nearly 650 acres along San Francisquito Creek, near Menlo Park. During the next decade he proceeded to acquire adjacent properties, until his holding surpassed eight thousand acres. Before there was Leland Stanford Junior University there was the Palo Alto Stock Farm. The fact is, the first passion of the founding president of the Central Pacific Railroad, governor of California, and later (1885–93) U.S. senator, was horses. In the final quarter of the nineteenth century, Leland Stanford's stock farm became a veritable laboratory for the scientific breeding and training of horses. Young Leland Junior was a capable rider who spent a good deal of time on horseback at his father's stock farm. Today Stanford University is still affectionately known as "the Farm."

The Palo Alto Stock Farm achieved its greatest renown in the years between 1880 and 1891. Governor Stanford's priority was to develop speed in trotters, horses that pulled a wheeled cart called a sulky in the harness races that were so popular at the time. What became known as Stanford's "Palo Alto system" pioneered the idea of training colts as yearlings instead of as adults, and driving horses at full speed for short runs instead of the then-standard practice of running longer distances at slower speeds. Also, Stanford favored the use of carrots over sticks: in other words, whips were put aside in favor of kindness and encouragement.

In the 1880s the Palo Alto Stock Farm set nineteen consecutive world records, thanks mainly to a stallion named Electioneer, often called the "world champion sire of world champions." Stanford purchased the stallion, against all advice, in 1877 for $12,000. In the course of the next fourteen years Electioneer sired 166 colts, all of which could trot a mile in under two and a half minutes. Electioneer fathered nine of the thirteen world-record champions bred in Palo Alto!

The Palo Alto Stock Farm was also the site of photographic experiments that Governor Stanford commissioned, allegedly to prove his theory that at one point in its fastest gait a trotter has all four feet off the ground. These experiments, conducted by Eadweard Muybridge, helped inspire the idea of moving pictures. (The restoration of the Stanford Mansion in Sacramento begun in the 1990s was aided by photos Muybridge took of the mansion in 1872.) Muybridge developed a technique that enabled him to take a sequence of consecutive images, using a battery of twenty-four cameras fitted with electro-shutters, that captured a trotter's movement. The experiment became the subject of a classic book published in 1881 titled *A Horse in Motion*, with an introduction by Governor Stanford.

I have to say I've never accepted that Stanford undertook this experiment in order to prove a bet that all four legs of a horse leave the ground. Hav-

Images of the
Eadweard Muybridge
"moving picture"
experiment as they
appeared in the
January 1901 issue
of *Sunset*.

ing grown up with horses, I could see with my own eyes that when a horse is running, there are times when all four of its feet are off the ground. So I just can't believe that was the reason for all of that effort and expense. More interesting to me is how this fits into a long history of Leland Stanford's concern with investigating and documenting the productivity of horses.

As a railroad man, Stanford had a special interest in the subject. There was no railroad in the world to compare with the transcontinental American railroad in the mid-nineteenth century. It opened up whole new regions for settlement, where you drove cattle to railheads, and you had branch railroads, starting with the Rio Grande and later the Great Northern and the Santa Fe. With this burst of growth came the increased need to reach satellite communities sprouting up in the interior. And the only way to do it back then was by horse, a critical method of transportation.

Stanford's keen interest in these matters stemmed in part from his responsibilities as director of Wells Fargo & Company, a position he occupied almost without interruption from 1870 until his death in June 1893. How long a Pony Express rider could ride a horse, how long a Wells Fargo draft horse could pull a heavy load, whether you needed four or six horses, which breeds worked best, what types of feed best served a horse's productivity—these kinds of problems led to some highly scientific analyses of horses in those days, similar to those we later applied to automobiles and airplanes. That's what Leland Stanford was into, and for me it's the most fascinating aspect of *A Horse in Motion*.

Leland Stanford's stock farm was officially closed in 1903. Stanford's horses were sold off to help finance the university. At a founder's day ceremony in 1918, President David Starr Jordan, referring to this sale, spoke of "the horses that saved the University"—no doubt in exaggeration. As the stock farm faded into history, the university expanded onto the old racetrack with a golf course, a driving range, and a student dormitory complex fittingly called Governor's Corner. The magnificent Red Barn, built between 1878 and 1880 as the training stable, is the last remaining original structure of the stock farm. In the spring of 1946, Stanford president Donald Tresidder, an ardent horseman, reopened the Red Barn as an equestrian facility.

I graduated from Stanford in 1942, but my connection to Don Tresidder went back to my days as a packer in Yosemite. In the early part of the century, small organized camps had sprouted up throughout the Yosemite Valley. One of these was known as Camp Curry, after the late David Curry, a onetime minister and sometime teacher from Indiana. Curry became something of a legend in Yosemite, mostly on the strength of his booming voice, which could be heard throughout the valley bellowing, "All's well!" It was Curry who introduced the famous Yosemite firefall: the burning embers sent splashing down the face of Glacier Point.

Don Tresidder was hired as camp porter at Camp Curry before the First World War. He enrolled at Stanford, although the war interrupted his education. It was at Yosemite that he met and fell in love with Mary Curry, younger daughter of David and Jennie. By then David Curry had died, leaving "Mother Curry," as she was called, to run things. Tresidder, meanwhile, had moved up the ladder from porter to assistant manager of Camp Curry. In 1925 Camp Curry merged with its chief rival, the Yosemite National Park Company, to form the Yosemite Park & Curry Company, with Tresidder as its first president. Tresidder's first big task was to oversee the construction of the Ahwahnee Hotel, which opened in 1927, the same year Tresidder received his medical degree from Stanford.

I enter the picture, in a modest way, in the late 1930s, when I went to Yosemite and packed supplies into the High Sierra camps. It was a summer job, and I was the junior man at the stable (the kind of humble-beginnings story I enjoyed recalling three decades later, when I served on the board

Bill Lane in Yosemite in the late 1930s.

Opposite, top:
Left to right: Mel,
Laurence, and Bill
Lane, at Rancheros
Visitadores, in Santa
Barbara in 1961.
Photo by Les Walsh.

Opposite, bottom:
Left to right:
Laurence, Mel, and
Bill Lane, 1950s.

of the Yosemite Park & Curry Company). Dr. and Mrs. Tresidder rode a lot, usually on the weekends, and they had some beautiful horses. I was not in charge of them, but I helped take care of them and would sometimes saddle them up for the Tresidders.

I often helped organize the children's burro picnic. We would gather at Camp Curry, and Mother Curry would sometimes come down from her little cottage and see us off. Mother Curry, who did all the cooking and administered the camps, was a very close friend of a Señora Lindeman, a Spanish lady who had married a German in Mexico and had three beautiful singing daughters, who became somewhat famous as the Lindeman Sisters.

One of the Lindeman daughters was Coco, a beautiful brunette a little older than I was, and I liked her very much. Coco played the guitar, and the sisters used to sing "Indian Love Call" for firefall, and I would call fire-fall—shouting the command "Let the fire fall!" from the valley floor to the fire-tenders two thousand feet up on Glacier Point. Quite often the sisters sang while the fire was falling. Coco was the hostess on the children's burro picnic, and I was the packer and mountain guide, and so we became close friends. And in fact we were able to remain good friends, because she later had a home in Portola Valley.

Horses continued to be part of my life in Portola Valley—and Jean's as well. Growing up in Iowa, I had "Betty"; growing up in Illinois, Jean had chestnut-colored "Red." Riding has given me a special connection to my daughter Brenda, an avid equestrian whose horse growing up was

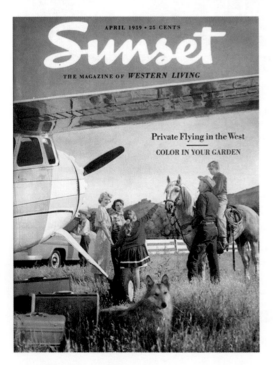

Sunset, April 1959.

called "Whiskey." Brenda, my neighbor on Westridge Drive in Portola Valley, owns two horses, while Jean and I have three.

I shared a love of horses and great riding experiences with my father and brother. Dad and Mel and I belonged to the Rancheros riding club, in Santa Barbara. Every year, the three of us, together with other horsemen, would ride out of Santa Barbara. This was usually the first weekend of May, and we'd ride for a week, covering some sixty miles. Those were wonderful bonding experiences, between father and brothers, and, after Dad's last ride, between the "Lane boys."

My dad's love of horses and horseback riding was a major factor behind his acquisition of Quail Hollow Ranch in the 1930s. In 1948, my parents added a complex of stables

Bill atop Friars Top Tuck ("Toppy") at the Stanford stables in 1997.

and barns with a large riding area. This led to Quail Hollow's only appearance in *Sunset*. The August 1948 issue published an article titled "A Report on Western Stables." One sentence in that article struck a chord with me: "When a barn works smoothly, when there's a place for everything, when both horses and men find it a pleasant place, it becomes the center of activity." I could have written those lines myself.

My own moment in the spotlight came a quarter century later, when *Western Horseman*, my favorite magazine next to *Sunset* (and one I tried to purchase over the years) published a feature on my Westridge stables in its February 1972 issue. The article spotlighted Cliff May's ingenious design of the stable—separate utilities installed, heavier foundation put in, walls and ceiling insulated—which gave us the option to convert the stable into a private home if we decided we wanted to do so at some future time. The stable was built on a separate lot, and all residential setback requirements were followed. This meant we could sell our own house without having to sell a large stable with it, not an attraction to most potential buyers.

Another innovation highlighted by *Western Horseman* was our safety features. Our daughter Brenda, ten years old at the time, handled most of the feeding duties, and we were aware that horses are not always on their best behavior at feeding time. Cliff May's design made it possible for the horses in the box stalls to be fed without people having to enter the stalls.

My twin background as a Stanford man and a horseman compelled me, in the early 1980s, to serve as chairman of the whirlwind campaign to save Stanford's historic Red Barn, which had been about to collapse for lack of maintenance. I teamed up with the operator of the barn's riding school and stable and with Stanford administrators to raise the necessary $950,000. I gave a lead gift and led a campaign to raise half a million dollars, a goal we achieved, and surpassed, within six weeks. Altogether some two hundred individuals, foundations, and businesses pitched in. After restoration and renovation, the Red Barn, a beautiful Victorian structure emblematic of the farmland origins of Stanford University, was reopened in April 1984.

As a finishing touch, in 2001 I donated to the university a statue of the legendary stallion Electioneer, which stands in front of the Red Barn.

Over the years I have continually championed the importance of horses in preserving and maintaining the rural environments that still exist on the peninsula. And so when the idea to restore the Folger Estate Stable in Wunderlich Park, in nearby Woodside, began to germinate, the fledgling committee turned to me. The Folger Estate

Bill Lane at his Cascade Lake retreat, circa 2005.

Stable was designed by Arthur Brown, Jr., the architect of numerous landmark structures in San Francisco and on the Stanford campus, including the Hoover Tower. It was another call to ride to the rescue. I gave the lead gift in order to get that campaign rolling, and I continued to provide considerable financial support to keep the project going.

Men and Mountains

Yosemite has remained my passion. Of all the philanthropic endeavors I've contributed to, the most meaningful to me has been the restoration of Glacier Point. I was involved in the effort to restore the natural habitat, redo the trails, and build an amphitheater for lectures and for stargazing. I love the coast, the Oregon coast in particular, but I would never take a beach recreation second home, or retirement home, over a mountain home. Jean and I have our mountain retreat at Cascade Lake in south Lake Tahoe, a house designed for us by Henrik Bull.

On the wall behind my desk in my Menlo Park office hangs the relief map of the West that my father once used. Every time I look at it I'm reminded that it's the mountains that create the climates and create the water reservoirs and lakes. They, above all, make for a different way of life out West. It's the mountains that trap the weather, that create the recreation, and shape the Western lifestyle. Historically it was the mountains that were the barrier to migration.

Sunset magazine through the years paid special attention to the mountains, as a place for vacation, meditation, escape. I think this coverage of the mountains was a conscious reflection of *Sunset*'s commitment to the West, because the mountains are what made the West different. There is the beach experience, of course, and the desert is unique too, and *Sunset* has certainly covered both the beach and the desert over the years. But the mountains set the tone for the West, and they received pride of place in *Sunset*.

Something of that spirit was captured by Sam Walter Foss, a New England librarian and journalist who in 1894 wrote a Fourth of July poem about the West titled "The Coming American." (It inspired a wonderful book of the same name by Irving Stone.) It is best known for its opening stanza:

> Bring me men to match my mountains,
> Bring me men to match my plains,
> Men with empires in their purpose,
> And new eras in their brains.

Stanford historian and my good friend David Kennedy has characterized these lines as "a notorious specimen of nineteenth-century screaming-eagle fustian"—meaning bombast. As he notes, Wallace Stegner improved on Foss by calling on Westerners to build "a society to match the scenery." Those words neatly capture the spirit behind the creation of the Bill Lane Center for the American West, which I founded in 2002 at Stanford University, with Professor Kennedy as co-director.

The Bill Lane Center is an interdisciplinary institute dedicated to enriching Western scholarship and spurring new and fruitful conversations about the past, present, and future of the West, broadly understood: from Canada to Mexico, from the Great Plains to the Pacific Rim. The goal of the center, where scholars, policymakers, journalists, and civic leaders come together to collaborate, is to make Stanford a leading regional citizen by establishing the center as the premier venue for the study of the North American West.

Sunset, June 1934.

Just before my ninetieth birthday, I attended our annual Bill Lane Center reception for returning interns, where I entertained all with what one participant described as a "decidedly full-throated" rendition of the "Let the fire fall!" command that as a young Yosemite Park employee I used to call out from the valley floor beneath Glacier Point. On days off, I would hike up the face of Glacier Point, where the burning embers were slowly pushed over the edge to become the spectacular firefall. The Yosemite firefall has long since been discontinued due to concerns over safety and the environment, but firefall nostalgia lives on, and no one ever tried to stop me from occasionally *calling* firefall.

Over the years, in conversation and in public talks, I have often mentioned the influence on me and Mel of our first visit to Yosemite, on a fam-

Bill Lane speaks at an award ceremony for Jean Lane at Northwestern University in 1997.

ily vacation in the summer of 1929: the unforgettable experience for two
Iowa farm boys of coming around the top of the lower valley, high on the
north side, along the Old Big Oak Flat Road, and suddenly seeing Bridal
Veil Falls on our right, El Capitan on our left, and Half Dome in the distance. Visitors heading into the valley on the Old Big Oak Flat Road (now
Highway 120) are often taken by surprise at this dramatic first view of the
valley, and until recently many missed the turnout for this, their first opportunity to catch a glimpse of Half Dome rising from the valley.

In 2009, the Yosemite Fund, the primary nonprofit fund-raising organization for Yosemite, which I have supported since its inception in 1988,
made a major commitment to Yosemite with a grant for the rehabilitation
of the area to be called Half Dome Overlook. In 2010 The Yosemite Fund
and Yosemite Association merged to form Yosemite Conservancy. This
project will both protect and restore the site while making it a better—and
safer—experience for the thousands of visitors each year who make this
their first stop within Yosemite.

Half Dome Overlook will feature a plaque to Mel and me, in honor of
Lane family support for the project, and also as a tribute to the life-chang-
ing experience of seeing this view of Half Dome for the first time in that
unforgettable summer of 1929. I know that Mel, who passed away in July
2007, would be immensely proud of the association.

Bill Lane at Yosemite circa 2003.

Epilogue

Promises to Keep

When *Sunset* moved from San Francisco to its new headquarters in Menlo Park in 1951, I suggested to my father that the company host a Christmas party for staff and their children. "But who will play Santa?" my father asked, quickly declining the role of Old Saint Nick. I said I would find the right person, and after giving it some thought, I decided I should play Santa myself. I rented a suit and used a pillow to fill out my tummy.

It turned out that I really loved being Santa. I love relating to kids and hearing what they have to say. For the next fifty-seven years I played Santa Claus, first for Christmas parties at *Sunset*, and since 1990 at the Ladera shopping center, on Alpine Road in Portola Valley. For *Sunset* parties I would arrive on horseback or by buggy, police car, a huge four-door Lincoln convertible, and even one time by helicopter.

When I served as U.S. ambassador to Australia, Jean and I hosted a festive and memorable Christmas party at the embassy residence in Canberra in 1988, Australia's bicentennial. Jean, an accomplished pianist, played the piano for the sing-along and orchestrated the instrumental chorus for some Christmas carols. Following a Lane family tradition, guests received a bamboo musical instrument from Thailand, called an *angklung*, which they shook when the appropriate number appeared on a piece of poster board.

These past several years in Portola Valley, Santa always arrives by fire engine, greeted by hundreds of children and their families over the course of two very busy hours. He listens to their wishes, checks their lists, and also uses the opportunity to offer some gentle advice. "Santa Claus watches very closely to see what you do," he tells them. "Do you help around the house? Your parents do a lot for you, and what do you do for them?" Santa also reminds them, "We live in a beautiful country, and we have to take care of it. When you're out on a trail, hiking or just walking down the street, if you see trash, you should pick it up." The wish lists have certainly evolved over the years, from little red wagons to the latest iPhone. Being a wise man,

167

Santa tells the children that while he cannot guarantee he will bring them everything they want, he promises to try.

When I was asked to share some of my thoughts about angels at a Christmas Eve service at our church in 1992, I talked about how we are reminded each December that angels and Christmas are inseparable—as evidenced by everything from Christmas carols to stained-glass church windows. Since then, I have looked into the matter and I've become aware how often "angels" are part of the conversation in our everyday lives all year long. Especially in America, the religious origins of angels have become blurred by the wide use of the word to name or describe, for example, a baseball team, a major metropolitan city, a well-behaved child, even a cake—and according to one dictionary definition, "a wealthy man easily separated from his money."

For centuries, artists and writers and others have depicted angels not only as messengers of God's word, but also in the context of good tidings brought by an "angel" who touched our lives with comfort, forgiveness, inspiration, and, most of all, love—perhaps in the person of a new friend, a doctor, a nurse, a wife, a husband, a minister, or a child. I think many people at one time or another believe they have a guardian angel, which is very definitely a biblical concept. Some of us even see ourselves in the role of angel—although, being honest, and also with the Bible as my point of reference, I think it is fair to say that most of us can be "devils" at times as well as "angels."

Santa Claus (Bill Lane, age 90) and a new friend at the Ladera shopping center in Portola Valley in December 2009.

The Lane family at Quail Hollow Ranch in November 2005, on the occasion of Bill's 86th birthday.

What I have learned from my experiences over the course of my long life has convinced me that the presence of "angels" in our personal lives is very much a matter of our individually recognizing some divine guidance from our maker, or some unexplained "message" represented by a blessed event: a very special wish-come-true, a loving relationship, an act of forgiveness, or a revelation for a new or more positive outlook on life that comes from a beautiful sunrise or sunset—in other words, something that cannot be explained by pure logic.

Beyond angels and my devoted parents and my caring teachers, I have had many strong winds at my back—people to support me, encourage me, challenge me, and disagree with me. My brother, Mel, played all these roles from my earliest years. I always admired Mel, but the determination, patience, and pure guts he displayed in the last years of his life deepened my admiration and affection for him. His long bout with illness could never extinguish the twinkle in his eyes. I married a wonderful lady with accomplishments of her own who has loved and supported me for more than fifty-five years. Jean and our very loving children and grandchildren have always been there for me, especially in my sunset years.

Index of Names

Rockefeller, Nelson, 129
Rogers, Will, 29, 41
Roosevelt, Eleanor, 140
Roosevelt, Theodore, xv, 21, 97, 98–99
Royston, Robert, 71

Schirra, Wally, 21
Shulman, Julius, 74
Shultz, George P., 136, 139, 148
Simon, William E., 134
Stanford, Jane Lathrop, 154
Stanford, Leland, 7, 151, 154, 155, 156
Stanford, Leland, Jr., 154, 155
Starr, Kevin, 13, 15, 23, 67, 151, 152
Stegner, Wallace, 112, 115, 162
Steinbeck, John, xix
Stephen, Sir Ninian, 137
Sterling, George, 10
Sterling, Wallace, 152
Stewart, Martha, 15

Tarkington, Booth, xii
Taylor, Frank J., 10
Taylor, Robert, 30
Thornton, Edmund B., 114
Train, Russell E., 133

Tresidder, Donald, 156, 157, 158

Udall, Stewart, 113

Vaughan, H. L., 73

Walker, Peter, 71
Wallace, DeWitt, 37
Warner, John, 127
Watt, James G., 116, 134
Weinberger, Caspar, 135, 139, 140
White, Stewart Edward, 10
Whitney, Josiah Dwight, 96–97
Wilbur, Ray Lyman, 33
Williams, Edward, 71
Williamson, Joe, 107
Willoughby, Howard, 37, 38, 39, 40, 41, 143
Wilson, Woodrow, 6, 91
Wirth, Conrad L., 119
Wright, Carleton H., 33, 34, 35, 36
Wright, Frank Lloyd, 63
Wright, Jim, 138
Wurster, William, 69

Yasukawa, Takeshi, 129
Young, James Webb, 25, 45

Zellerbach, Isadore, 25